PLANNING

YOUR MARRIAGE SERVICE

PLANNING

YOUR MARRIAGE SERVICE

CHRISTOPHER L. WEBBER

AND

MARGARET WEBBER

MOREHOUSE PUBLISHING
Harrisburg, PA

Copyright © 1992 by Christopher L. Webber and Margaret Webber

Morehouse Publishing

Editorial Office:
871 Ethan Allen Highway
Ridgefield, CT 06877

Corporate Office:
P.O. Box 1321
Harrisburg, PA 17105

Scripture quotations are from the New Revised Standard Version of the
Bible, copyright © 1989 by the Division of Christian Education of the
National Council of Churches of Christ in the U.S.A. Used by permission.

Library of Congress Cataloging-in-Publication Data
Webber, Christopher.
    Planning your marriage service / Christopher L. Webber and
Margaret Webber.
        p.   cm.
    ISBN: 0-8192-1590-2 (pbk.)
    1. Marriage service. I. Webber, Margaret. II. Title.
BV199.M3W43 1992   92-15257
265'.5—dc20   CIP

Printed in the United States of America
by
BSC Litho

CONTENTS

The suggested readings are drawn from the following sources. An asterisk indicates that the wording and spelling have been slightly changed to conform to modern usage or for inclusive language.

Augustine of Hippo, in *Readings for the Daily Office from the Early Church*, pp. 290-291, J. Robert Wright, ed., (New York: Church Hymnal Corporation, 1991). Used by permission.

Buechner, Frederick, *The Hungering Dark*, pp. 93-95. Copyright © 1969 by Frederick Buechner. Reprinted by permission of HarperCollins Publishers.

de Chardin, Teilhard, *The Hymn of the Universe*, p. 145. Copyright © 1961 by Editions de Seuil. English translation copyright © 1965 by William Collins Sons and Company, Ltd. and Harper and Row Publishers, Inc. Reprinted by permission of HarperCollins Publishers.

* Donne, John, *The Sermons of John Donne*, 10 Volumes, pp. 245-255, volume 3. Edited and translated by Evelyn Simpson and George Potter, copyright © 1953–1962 by Regents. Used by permission of the University of California Press.

* Julian of Norwich, *Revelations of Divine Love*, p. 9 and p. 169; edited by Dom Roger Hudleston, OSB, (London: Burns and Oates, Ltd., 1952). Used by permission.

King, Martin Luther, Jr., *The Strength to Love*, (New York: Walker and Company, 1985), © 1963, reprinted by permission of Joan Daves Agency.

L'Engle, Madeleine, *The Irrational Season*, pp. 46-48. Copyright © 1977 by Crosswicks Ltd. Reprinted by permission of HarperCollins Publishers.

Weil, Simone, *Waiting on God*, p. 85 and p. 93, (London: Fontana Books, 1959).

PART I: THE SERVICE

INTRODUCTION

Congratulations! Together you are beginning to plan what may well be the most important day of your life. Except for birth and death, when someone else normally does the planning, no change in our lives is as significant as the change from being single to being married. Here you have the one opportunity in your life to plan the statement of faith and commitment you want to make **and** to participate in it with the person who means the most to you, as well as with your family and friends.

The plans you make also involve more than just one day. They involve the days before and the days after. If you plan well, you will learn things that will affect your life now; you will look forward to the day itself with a greater understanding and deeper joy. And if you plan well, your married life will be affected; you will understand better how the love of God and God's people, the church, is a strength on which to depend. Good planning makes a real and lasting difference.

The service you are beginning to plan is one in which you **say** something and **do** something. What you **do** is enter into a new relationship, create a new family. You are changed by what you do. But you also **say** something. Your marriage service says something out loud to your friends and family about your love and your faith, and that will affect them also. What you **do** is not much affected by the choices you make about the service. The service will take place anyway and you will still be married whether the choices you make are good or bad. But what you **say** depends very much on your choices; if you choose well, others will hear about the love and joy you have found, share it more fully, and support you in living it out.

Perhaps, then, you should begin by spending some time thinking together about what it is you would like to say. You may want to make some notes on a piece of paper. What is it you feel about each other? What are the strengths you have found in each other and want to give to each other? What are your hopes for your marriage? Why is it important to you to be married in church? How important are your friends and family in your lives? And what does God's love mean to you? Where do you see God's love at work in your lives and the lives of others? When you can answer questions like these, it will be easier to make the choices that this book describes.

How to use this book

In the center of this book is a pull-out page which lets you check off the choices you make as you plan your service.[1] You might want to pull it out now and run it through a copier. Make two or three copies. Then you can make some initial decisions and perhaps change them later. When you are finished you can make a copy for the church to keep on file and keep one for yourselves.

But first read through this book slowly and carefully and talk about it with each other and with your friends and family. Pray about it, too: ask God's guidance in the choices you make. Especially in choosing readings, don't try to do it quickly. Read one or two passages a day with the commentary provided on the facing page, and then think about them and discuss them with others. We suggest that you start by looking at the gospel selections since the gospel, containing the words and actions of Jesus,

---

[1] This book assumes that you are using *The Book of Common Prayer, 1979*, of the Episcopal Church and staying within the choices offered there. We have assumed that alternatives offered in "An Order for Marriage" (pp. 435–436), such as a non-biblical reading, can also be offered within "The Celebration and Blessing of a Marriage" (pp. 423–432).

has always been given the place of honor. If your marriage includes the eucharist, the gospel is always read last for this reason.

Notice that each section of this book describes *one* of the choices you need to make and has a letter code. The pull-out sheet has the same letter code to show you where to enter that choice when you have made it.

Take your time. Half the fun is the planning. And remember that you have already made the most important decision by choosing each other!

Other matters you need to consider

No book can cover all the differences of architecture and policy in different churches. Be sure to discuss the following subjects with the priest (or deacon):[2]

1) *Service program.* Will it be helpful to your family and friends to give them a program, listing prayer book pages, hymn numbers, and names of participants, or even the complete text of the service with the readings? If you do this, you can insert directions for the congregation about when to stand or to be seated, and when to join in prayers or responses. Will you arrange for the printing yourselves, or ask if the church will take care of it? (If you do this, it is important to make your decisions well in advance of your wedding day, and to compensate the church for the expense.)

2) *Attendants.* What will be the number of ushers and bridesmaids, and where they will stand? Placement may be best arranged at the rehearsal but can also be discussed in advance with the priest.

3) *Flowers.* Policy as to what can be done and where flowers can be placed will differ from one church to

---

[2]This book uses the term "priest" although a deacon can also perform a marriage service. Since a deacon cannot preside at a eucharist and many weddings include a eucharist, it seems simpler to use the one term.

another. There may be also a recommendation or requirement about using a florist familiar with the church.

4) *Runner and candles.* If you want a runner for the church aisle, find out whether the church has one or whether you need to get one from the florist or caterer. If you want more than the usual candles, find out what is permitted and, if you have a florist provide candles, make sure they are guaranteed to be dripless or that protection for the floor is provided.

5) *Photography.* Many churches have strict rules about the use of flashbulbs during the service and what may or may not be done with video cameras and lights. Make sure that the professional photographer and your friends know the church's policy. If you have a program of the service printed for the congregation, you can include a sentence saying: "Please take NO flash pictures during the processions or the service."

6) *Costs.* Normally the church will have a set fee for the organist and sexton or custodian. There may be one inclusive fee to cover the expenses to the church of providing these services, as well as heat and light and maintenance. An honorarium for the priest is appropriate and generally is not included in the set fees.

7) *Other Requirements.* Don't forget that you need a marriage license. Get it well in advance (but not so long before that it expires!) and bring it to the church ahead of time. The priest will also tell you, if there has been a divorce, what you need to do to meet the church's requirements in this regard.

A. The Service

The first and most important choice you will make is whether or not to include the eucharist (Mass or Holy

Communion) in your marriage service. There are two important reasons for choosing to include the eucharist. The first is that God's greatest gift of love is the life of Jesus Christ which we receive at the altar in the bread and wine. God's gift of love strengthens you for the new life you are beginning. Secondly, the eucharist is the family meal of God's family. There is no better way to begin your life as a family, which will be centered around your family table, than to come to God's table to share in the Christian family meal.

Sometimes people will be concerned that non-Christian guests or members of other Christian churches will feel "left out" if they cannot come to the altar. But your friends will want you to receive all the gifts your church has to give and, even if they are not free to receive communion, they will be glad that you have not changed the service on their account. Others are sometimes concerned about making the service "too long." The difference in time will probably be less than half an hour and that seems a small investment of time to make when you think of the many years that lie ahead. Nevertheless, there are many factors that bear on this choice and you must make the choices that best fit your circumstances. If you decide not to have the eucharist as part of your service, perhaps you can have a service for yourselves and some of your friends and family earlier in the day. You can at least plan to receive communion together soon after the wedding and regularly thereafter.

B. Music

Nothing does more to set the feeling of joy at a wedding than the music. You will probably be asked to meet with the organist to discuss the music you would like to have. Before that meeting, you might want to think about the following possibilities:

1) *Prelude.* Usually the organist will begin to play fifteen minutes or more before the wedding. It is not

necessary to choose this music (and perhaps only your guests will hear it!), but if you like good music, you may want to make suggestions of music for this time. Good choices will help set the tone for the day.

2) *Entrance (and exit) music.* The first and last note for your wedding is set by the processional music. It should be strong and joyful. The organist will generally offer several suggestions to you, including both very familiar pieces and lesser known ones. She or he can also tell you about the context and history of each piece to help you make your choice. That choice, with the others you will be making, enhances your statement to the congregation about what your marriage service means to you. And afterwards you will always be able to hear that music and be reminded not just of *a* wedding but of *your* wedding.

3) *Hymns.* There are several places in the service where hymns can be used. They need not be "wedding hymns" (these are usually too unfamiliar to work well anyway). The best choices are familiar hymns that express God's love for us and the joy with which we praise God. A list of suggested hymns follows.

4) *Vocal or instrumental music.* You may have friends who are talented musicians who would be willing to sing or play at your wedding. The church organist can also arrange for special music. Such music before or during the service can add a special note, but it should not be overdone. Soloists, whether they are very good or not, can draw attention away from the two being married and "dominate" the service. All such music needs to be arranged both with the priest conducting the service and with the organist.

Suggested Hymns for Use at a Wedding

Number	First Line
302	Father, we thank thee†

---

†These hymns are especially appropriate if there is a eucharist.

336	Come with us, O blessed Jesus†
377	All people that on earth do dwell
380	From all that dwell below the skies
390	Praise to the Lord, the Almighty
397	Now thank we all our God
401	The God of Abraham praise
410	Praise, my soul, the King of heaven
460	Alleluia! sing to Jesus!
487	Come, my Way, my Truth, my Life
488	Be thou my vision
516	Come down, O Love divine
517	How lovely is thy dwelling place
522	Glorious things of thee are spoken
645	The King of love my shepherd is (*)
657	Love divine, all loves excelling
663	The Lord my God my shepherd is (*)
671	Amazing grace! how sweet the sound
686	Come, thou fount of every blessing
697	My God, accept my heart this day
707	Take my life, and let it be

(*) These hymns are both paraphrases of Psalm 23, and could be used instead of reading a psalm.

C. The Entrance

Many weddings begin with the groom and best man standing at the front of the church while the bridal procession comes down the aisle, the bride coming last on her father's arm. This custom is based on very old ideas about the bride as property, brought in by one man and led out by another. You may want to use the "traditional" entrance procession, or you might like to consider alternatives which express your relationships more accurately.

1) The groom and best man come to the front of the church and wait for the bridal procession. The ushers, then the bridesmaids, then the bride come down

---

†These hymns are especially appropriate if there is a eucharist.

the aisle. The bride is accompanied by her father or some other family member or friend. Flower girls and ring bearers may be included in the procession.

2) The bride and groom both come down the aisle in a procession which may be led by the priest and acolyte(s). Such a procession might begin with an acolyte or assistant carrying the cross, followed by the priest (and other clergy). Ushers follow them, and then the groom, accompanied by his parents and/or by the best man. Then the bridesmaids come, followed by the bride, accompanied by her parents and/or the maid of honor.

The second pattern is intended to express better the equality of the bride and groom and the support of their families.

3) There will be also very small or informal weddings at which the bride and groom will come down the aisle together, led by their witnesses and, perhaps, by acolytes and clergy.

D. The Presentation (optional)

1) A generation or two ago, it was customary for the bride's father to escort her down the aisle and stand between her and the groom through the opening statements. Then the priest said, "Who giveth this woman to be married to this man?" and the father gave the bride's hand to the priest, who gave it to the groom. Originally this represented the carrying out of a contract between families and even between tribes.

2) In a modern version, the priest would ask, "Who presents this woman to be married to this man?" The bride's father (or other presenter) would then respond, (2a) "I do," or, (2b) "Her mother and I do." The father would then usually give his daughter a kiss and step back to stand with his wife.

3) For a more complete expression of family support

the priest might be asked to say, "Who presents this man and this woman to be married to each other?" The bride's escort would then say, (3a) "I do." Alternatively, (3b) the parents or escorts of both bride and groom might respond together: "We present John and Mary to be married to each other." Or, (3c) the parents or escorts of the bride and groom might respond separately: "We present John to be married to Mary," and "We present Mary to be married to John." If parents or others have come down the aisle with the bride and groom, they might stand at the front of the church until they have made this response and then step back to their places in the congregation.

4) Another common pattern is for the bride's escort to walk with her to the front of the church, give her a kiss, give her hand to the groom, and step back into the congregation to relax and enjoy the ceremony.

The first three variations would normally come after the opening statements. The fourth alternative would come before the opening statements are made.

E. The Ministry of the Word (p. 426)

This is the second major phase of the ceremony. The first stage consists of public statements of the meaning of marriage and your readiness to make the marriage commitment. Now, in the second stage, we hear the teaching of the Bible (and, perhaps, wisdom from other sources) concerning marriage. The choices you make here may take the most time just because there are so many possibilities. Here especially you have the opportunity to make choices that reflect your own love for each other and your understanding of God's gift of love to you. As you read the Bible and make your selections, bear in mind the questions asked in the Introduction: consider God's love for you, your love for each other, and the church, families, and communities that support you with their love.

The Bible is the primary resource in choosing readings since it is God's word to us about love. Love has to do with choosing and giving. We know this from our own experience, but that experience needs to be shaped and guided by the centuries of Jewish and Christian experience and by the life of Jesus, the supreme example of self-giving love. The following pages will suggest various appropriate readings and will comment on their value. You are not limited to these readings and should feel free to consider others that have special meaning for you.

It is also possible, with the consent of the priest, to choose readings from non-biblical sources. But choose carefully: many familiar passages about love are inadequate expressions of Christian love. They are self-centered rather than self-giving and focus too much on the romantic and emotional aspects of love. Remember also that poetry often packs too much thought into too few words to be understood easily on first hearing. Shakespeare's Sonnet 116, for example, says some very good things but requires more careful study than is possible in the midst of a church service. The readings should express the understanding that our love and joy is a gift and has a purpose larger than our own happiness.

Think of this section of the service as made up of alternating layers of readings and hymns or psalms: after each reading it is useful to have a psalm or hymn so that there is time to think about it before the next begins. There are two main options:

1) If the service includes a celebration of the eucharist, there must be at least two readings, and one of these readings must be from the gospels. One or two additional readings can be chosen from the Old Testament or the other books of the New Testament, or, with the consent of the priest, from a non-biblical source. Each reading can be followed by a hymn or psalm. Here are some of the patterns you could follow:

a. First Reading:_____
   (Psalm or hymn: _____)
   Second Reading:_____
   (Psalm or hymn: _____)
   Gospel Reading:_____

b. First Reading:_____
   (Psalm or hymn: _____)
   Gospel Reading:_____

2) If the service does not include a celebration of the eucharist, there needs to be at least one reading from the Bible, but you can choose one or two additional readings if you wish. The other readings, with the consent of the priest, could be chosen from a non-biblical source. Each reading can be followed by a hymn or psalm.

c. (First Reading: _____)
   (Psalm or hymn: _____)
   (Second Reading:_____)
   (Psalm or hymn: _____)
   Bible Reading:_____

NOTE: It is good to involve family members and friends in the liturgy by asking them to read one or two of the lessons. At a eucharist, the priest (or a deacon) must read the Gospel selection but other selections may be read by any competent readers. Be sure that they have studied the reading ahead of time and, if possible, practiced reading it in the church. Note your choice of readings and readers on the pull-out sheet.

The psalms can be read in unison by the congregation or responsively between the congregation and a reader (another opportunity to involve a friend or family member).

Psalms appropriate for use at a wedding are the following: 23, 67, 127, 128, 150.

Response to the Readings

Usually the readings will be followed by a homily, a short sermon based on the readings you have chosen. It would be helpful for you to discuss with the priest your reasons for selecting the lessons and the themes you would like to emphasize. Talk with the priest about where you can sit during the readings and homily. Placing chairs for the wedding party may not be easy, but it may be even more difficult to maneuver into a pew in a wedding dress!

After the homily, you may wish to say together the Apostles' Creed to affirm your belief in the God who unites us in love. The Apostles' Creed is a more personal statement than the longer Nicene Creed, and therefore more appropriate in the marriage service. The Apostles' Creed also will probably be more familiar to non-Episcopalians. If you elect to say one of the Creeds you will want to have the text written out in the program or be sure people have Prayer Books available and are given a page number.

F. The Marriage (p. 427)

1) *The procession to the altar.* The exchange of vows will normally take place in front of the altar. In some churches the first part of the wedding takes place at the choir step and the wedding party then moves to the altar rail for the exchange of vows. In other churches, there is no separation between the congregation and altar and the whole ceremony is held at the same place. If there is a procession to the altar, this is a good place for a hymn or other music.

2) *The exchange of vows.* The words themselves are not optional. They are the oldest part of the service; some phrases can be traced back to Anglo-Saxon poetry over a thousand years old. They sum up the inclusive open-endedness of marriage ("for better *for* worse", not "for better *or* worse"—both are a normal part of any marriage) and the lifelong commitment.

They may be repeated after the priest, read from a book or card, or recited from memory.

> a. To repeat the vows after the priest is certainly the least stressful way. It has the further advantage of demonstrating that none of us "invents" marriage; God created marriage and establishes the terms which we now freely accept.

> b. To recite the vows from memory puts the emphasis on our own deep commitment. God may have established the terms of marriage but we have made them our own and speak them from the heart. (And the priest is always there to prompt if memory fails!)

> c. To read the vows is a compromise—and probably not a good one. It may provide the appearance of speaking for oneself without prompting, but it is hard to read a card or book while looking at one's partner.

3) *The exchange of rings.* The giving of a ring has always symbolized the sharing of possessions and for that reason the ring is usually gold or silver. When the man was the sole wage-earner, it made sense to have a single ring. In a day when both partners are usually working outside the home, it is appropriate for the man and woman to exchange rings. (NOTE: Other appropriate symbols may be exchanged instead of, or in addition to rings.)

G. The Prayers (pp. 428-430)

One of the reasons to come to church for a wedding is to ask God's help in living out your marriage vows. The prayers provided here are for that purpose. And the first prayer offered is the one Jesus taught his disciples and which all Christians use. You are given a choice between the old and new versions of that prayer.

The prayer on pp. 429-430 of the Prayer Book asks not only that you will be given the guidance and strength you will need, but that others may be helped by your love and guided by your example.

The Prayer Book says that "one or more" of the prayers may be omitted if there is not a Communion. Perhaps, then, the whole prayer could be omitted if there were no Communion and some other prayer or prayers could be substituted. The petitions of the prayer provided follow a logical sequence from prayers for you, the couple, to prayer for your friends and the larger society, and it is hard to see why any of them (except the one for children) would be omitted unless some other prayer were being substituted. The prayer for children would probably be omitted if the couple being married is beyond childbearing years.

H. The Blessing of the Marriage (pp. 430-431)

Christian marriage is a many-sided relationship. It is made not just by a man and woman coming together, but by a man and woman coming together in God's presence with a priest and a congregation of their friends. The fact that it takes place in church symbolizes this; so does the fact that the priest joins their hands; and so do the various people who participate in each part of the service. Nevertheless, the blessing is a high point in the service and emphasizes God's role in a Christian marriage. A Christian marriage is not lived by our own strength but by the grace of God. Therefore the bride and groom kneel and the priest pronounces God's blessing, asking that they may live together faithfully in this life and find in their marriage a foretaste of the eternal life we are promised.

There is a choice of two prayers before the blessing itself.

Prayer 1: This prayer uses more ornate language than Prayer 2. It speaks of Jesus as the example of Christian life and of the gift of the Holy Spirit to empower us. God's love is compared to a "seal" (the wedding rings), a "mantle" (the wedding garments), and a "crown" (a symbol used in Orthodox Christian weddings). The reference to the saints who "feast for ever in your heavenly home" reminds us of the link between the sharing of the eucharist, the joy of the marriage feast, and the promise of eternal life.

Prayer 2: In this prayer we return to the language of the opening address in which Christian marriage is compared to the "unity between Christ and his Church." God is asked to give the married couple such "faithfulness and patience, in wisdom and true godliness, that their home may be a haven of blessing and peace."

I. The Peace (optional) (p. 431)

As in a Sunday morning eucharist, the Peace marks a turning point in the service. Now that you, the bride and groom, are husband and wife, you may exchange a kiss as a sign of love and peace and unity. It is appropriate for you to be the ones who extend that sign of love and peace to others. It is easy and natural to turn and give a hug or kiss or handshake to the bridesmaids and ushers standing near you. Depending on the location of the altar, the size of the congregation, and the length of the bride's dress, it may be harder to go out to your families and the congregation and exchange the peace with them. This might be a time for a solo, a hymn or other music as the peace is exchanged and the joy which is expressed by bride and groom is radiated out to their friends and family.

If there is no celebration of the eucharist, you might prefer to exchange the Peace immediately before the Lord's Prayer (p. 428), and the service ends following the Blessing.

J. The Offertory (p. 432)

Now the joy of the marriage ceremony is expressed in the celebration of the eucharist. We gather at God's table to share the feast in which Christ himself is present with us. Now you will share your first meal as husband and wife and receive God's gift of love and strength.

It is appropriate for you to present the bread and wine and water that will be used at this service. If baking is one of your skills, you might even have made the loaf to be used. You can discuss with the priest how to arrange the presentation of the gifts. If the bread and wine are usually brought from the back of the church, you may want to do it that same way. Perhaps you will have walked down the aisle exchanging the peace and can now come back to the altar bringing the bread and the wine. Or, if that is complicated, perhaps a small table can be placed near the altar and you can go there to get the bread and wine and water to offer.

K. The Eucharistic Prayer

Since the marriage service is phrased in contemporary language, you will probably want to continue the service with Rite II and choose one of the four eucharistic prayers in that Rite. If you prefer to continue with Rite I and traditional language, there are two eucharistic prayers from which to choose. All these prayers contain a wide variety of images and have deep roots in Christian history. To choose among them is not easy, but you may be able to emphasize important aspects of your marriage by your selection. *Notice that the "Proper Preface for Marriage" is incorporated in Prayers A and B but not in Prayers C and D.*

Eucharistic Prayer A (p. 361 ff.). Commonly used on Sunday mornings, this is probably the eucharistic prayer most familiar to Episcopalians. The reference to "unity, constancy, and peace" seems especially important at a marriage, and the prayer to "bring us with all your saints into the joy of your eternal kingdom" makes the connection again between the joy we are given here and the joy we are promised hereafter.

Eucharistic Prayer B (p. 367 ff.). Similar in many ways to Prayer A, this prayer seems to give more prominence to the coming of Jesus into the world and the change he makes in Christian lives. There is also an even stronger emphasis on the final joy we are promised.

Eucharistic Prayer C (p. 369 ff.). The most "different" of the eucharistic prayers, Prayer C places a very strong emphasis on the creation and environment and our unity with those who have served God in every age. This prayer also allows much more participation for the congregation.

Eucharistic Prayer D (p. 372 ff.). Drafted by an ecumenical committee including Roman Catholic, Anglican, and Protestant scholars, this prayer has been approved for use in Lutheran and Methodist churches and might be a good choice if the bride and groom come from different Christian traditions. Special emphases in this prayer are on the goodness and love God shows us and on God's love for the poor and the powerless. There is also a point in the prayer at which special intercessions can be included. You might like to mention the names of departed members of both families or those unable to be present because of sickness.

L. The Communion

The service comes to a climax in the sharing of the "Bread of Life" and the "Cup of Salvation." It would be a wonderful sign of unity and sharing of love if everyone present could come to the altar and share this special meal with you. All baptized persons are welcome at the altar in the Episcopal Church and you may want to urge them to come by either a printed or spoken invitation.

You should discuss this aspect of the service with the priest and decide whether such a general invitation is possible. Sometimes there are differences of church membership or of religion within the families involved or among your friends, so that a general invitation would cause division rather than unity. If so, perhaps you will want to limit communion to the attendants or immediate family.

The time element is sometimes mentioned as an obstacle but it doesn't need to be one. Many parishes have lay members licensed to assist with the ministration of communion who will be happy to assist if given sufficient notice. Don't let yourself feel rushed. This is your moment, and if it takes an hour instead of forty-five minutes, that simply gives you more time to enjoy and absorb what is happening!

M. The Postcommunion Prayer, Dismissal, and Procession

The service ends with the postcommunion prayer, dismissal, and procession.

1) The Postcommunion Prayer (p. 432) gives thanks for the unity we are given in the eucharist and prays that the unity of marriage may bring us at last to perfect and eternal unity with the God who created us for that final purpose.

2) There is a choice of four dismissal sentences (p. 366). The second ("Go in peace to love and serve the Lord") is an excellent summary of the meaning of Christian marriage. But the first, which emphasizes our relationship with Christ, the third, which emphasizes the power of the Holy Spirit, and the fourth, which expresses our thankfulness to God, all have something to commend them. You should choose the one which seems to carry out most fully the shape

you have chosen to give the service as a whole.

3) The final procession from the altar will usually be accompanied by triumphant music. Remember that marriage is always a process, a procession, in which we continue to develop and change and move on to new places to serve God and each other in new ways. Your marriage will, with God's grace, continue to develop through the reception and honeymoon, through all the years of your life on this earth, and finally in the ultimate joy and unity of the eternal marriage feast to which God calls us.

PART II: THE READINGS

On the following pages are readings appropriate for a Christian marriage. Remember that you are free to consider other possibilities but should always consult with the priest who is presiding. We have provided some comments about the readings which we hope will not only help you make your choices but also help you see more clearly some of the wider meaning of what you are about to do.

The readings have been printed one to a page and in a larger type so that you can run the page through a copier and simply give it to the person doing the reading. If the copier can enlarge the printed text, so much the better.

Additional Suggested Readings

Old and New Testament
Genesis 2:4–9,15–24 (A man clings to his wife, and they become one flesh)

Ecclesiastes 3:1–11 (A time for every matter under heaven)

Jeremiah 31:31–32a,33–34a (I will put my law . . . in their hearts)

Romans 12:1–2, 9–13 (Let love be genuine)

Ephesians 3:14–19 (To know the love of Christ that surpasses knowledge)

Gospel
St. Matthew 5:13–16 (Let your light shine before others)

St. Matthew 7:21, 24–29 (Like a wise man who built his house on rock)

St. Matthew 22:35–40 (You shall love the Lord . . . with all your heart)

St. John 17:20–26 (That they all may be one)

Old Testament Reading 1

A Reading from the Book of Genesis   [1:26-31]

Then God said, "Let us make humankind in our image, according to our likeness; and let them have dominion over the fish of the sea, and over the birds of the air, and over the cattle, and over all the wild animals of the earth, and over every creeping thing that creeps upon the earth." So God created humankind in his image, in the image of God he created them; male and female he created them. God blessed them, and God said to them, "Be fruitful and multiply, and fill the earth and subdue it; and have dominion over the fish of the sea and over the birds of the air and over every living thing that moves upon the earth." God said, "See, I have given you every plant yielding seed that is upon the face of all the earth, and every tree with seed in its fruit; you shall have them for food. And to every beast of the earth, and to every bird of the air, and to everything that creeps on the earth, everything that has the breath of life, I have given every green plant for food." And it was so. God saw everything that he had made, and indeed, it was very good. And there was evening and there was morning, the sixth day.

The Word of the Lord.

Indeed It Was Very Good

The story of creation is a really good one with which to begin a marriage. You are sharing with God in creating something brand new. Perhaps only when you have a child do you have the feeling as strongly as at a wedding that everything is sparkling fresh and new.

But there's much more to the story than that. Notice how it says, ". . . in the image of God he created them; male and female he created them." First, it's amazing to learn that we are made in God's image, that we are like God in essential ways. But, secondly, we notice that the image of God is "male and female." God is neither male nor female but within the being of God are characteristics that we tend to think of as being particularly masculine and feminine—though, in truth, each of us needs and has some of them all. God is strong, God is beautiful, God is powerful, God is compassionate. So we can think of God as including the best of both sexes, and both sexes as reflecting in varying measure the various aspects of God. When two human beings come together in love, uniting the gifts each is given, we see some central part of God's purpose in creation being fulfilled.

There's also much in this passage to reflect on in terms of our relationship to our world, our environment. God gives us dominion over creation, and that is both our problem and our challenge. We have the ability to destroy the world or to renew it. We see the power of love in a marriage and in the joy we share with our friends, but that sharing of love can't be limited to human beings; it needs to reach out and embrace all of creation so that we can see once again how good the world is which God made for us.

Old Testament Reading 2

A Reading from the Song of Songs [2:10-13, 8:6-7]

My beloved speaks and says to me: "Arise, my love, my fair one, and come away; for now the winter is past, the rain is over and gone. The flowers appear on the earth; the time of singing has come, and the voice of the turtledove is heard in our land. The fig tree puts forth its figs, and the vines are in blossom; they give forth fragrance. Arise, my love, my fair one, and come away."

Set me as a seal upon your heart, as a seal upon your arm; for love is strong as death, passion fierce as the grave. Its flashes are flashes of fire, a raging flame. Many waters cannot quench love, neither can floods drown it. If one offered for love all the wealth of his house, it would be utterly scorned.

The Word of the Lord.

Love is Strong as Death

The Song of Songs is not a familiar part of the Bible for most people. If you haven't read it before, you might try reading a chapter or two to get a "feel" for it. This is the most sensual book of the Bible, a poem of praise for the pleasure of physical love. Some people are shocked to find such poetry in the Bible, but the Bible depicts the whole world God made in all its aspects—and the physical expression of the love of a man and a woman for each other is surely an important part of this world.

The two brief sections here speak of the beauty of love and the power of love. You might choose either section, or both.

The first paragraph sets love in the context of the beauty of springtime. All life is renewed, flowers open, birds sing—and many people get married. Springtime and marriage both have to do with the beginning of new life. The joy and beauty of both are God's gift.

The second paragraph speaks of the power of love, comparing it to unquenchable fire. If your engagement has faced and overcome various obstacles, this may seem to express your experience. But notice also the danger in a "raging fire." Love can overcome many obstacles but love can also rage out of control like a forest fire. One value of the institution of marriage, especially Christian marriage, is that it provides us with a community for support and guidance so that the power of love can be channeled in constructive directions.

Old Testament Reading 3

A Reading from the Book of Isaiah.   [25:1,4a,6-9]

O LORD, you are my God; I will exalt you, I will praise your name; for you have done wonderful things, plans formed of old, faithful and sure. For you have been a refuge to the poor, a refuge to the needy in their distress, a shelter from the rainstorm and a shade from the heat. On this mountain the LORD of hosts will make for all peoples a feast of rich food, a feast of well-aged wines, of rich food filled with marrow, of well-aged wines strained clear. And he will destroy on this mountain the shroud that is cast over all peoples, the sheet that is spread over all nations; he will swallow up death forever. Then the Lord GOD will wipe away the tears from all faces, and the disgrace of his people he will take away from all the earth, for the LORD has spoken. It will be said on that day, Lo, this is our God; we have waited for him, so that he might save us. This is the LORD for whom we have waited; let us be glad and rejoice in his salvation.

The Word of the Lord.

A Feast for All People

This is the first text that speaks of God preparing a meal for the people of God—and it sounds like a marriage feast! This passage would fit well with the reading from Revelation (19:6-9) and the gospel passages from Matthew (22:1-14), Luke (24:13-35), or John (2:1-11), which also speak of a shared meal or a wedding feast. The Bible uses the picture of a wedding feast as one of the best ways to describe the love and care which God pours out on us and the joy with which that love is shared. Those who are planning a wedding will understand why this is such a good illustration of God's love. This passage from Isaiah speaks of joy, inclusion, and patience.

First, God's will for us is joy. The Prayer Book points this out at the beginning of the marriage service: "The union of husband and wife . . . is intended by God for their mutual joy." Joy and food go together. We seem to need to share a meal when we have good news to celebrate, and the sharing of a meal itself produces joy. How often have you been to a wedding that didn't begin in church and end at a reception or meal? Even though the wedding in church may include a sharing of food at God's table, we seem to need some further sharing of food afterward. Both the service and the feast are God's gift and a sharing of the joy God gives us.

Second, the feast is for "all people." You probably won't invite the whole world to your wedding reception, but you will probably invite as many as you can afford. But God can afford a feast without any limitation and seeks to draw all people into the kingdom. The more inclusive our sharing of food, the more like the feast in God's kingdom it will be.

Third, the feast involves waiting. Anything as elaborate as a wedding requires planning. We have to set a date months ahead and wait for it to come. Joy requires patience. So God has been at work since the beginning of the world working patiently to prepare us to be ready to share the feast. We may wonder sometimes why God doesn't give us everything good right now, but if we are planning a wedding we know the value of waiting until everything and everyone is ready.

New Testament Reading 1

**A Reading from the First Letter of
St. Paul to the Corinthians.** [13:1-13]

If I speak in the tongues of mortals and of angels, but do not have love, I am a noisy gong or a clanging cymbal. And if I have prophetic powers, and understand all mysteries and all knowledge, and if I have all faith, so as to remove mountains, but do not have love, I am nothing. If I give away all my possessions, and if I hand over my body so that I may boast, but do not have love, I gain nothing. Love is patient; love is kind; love is not envious or boastful or arrogant or rude. It does not insist on its own way; it is not irritable or resentful; it does not rejoice in wrongdoing, but rejoices in the truth. It bears all things, believes all things, hopes all things, endures all things. Love never ends. But as for prophecies, they will come to an end; as for tongues, they will cease; as for knowledge, it will come to an end. For we know only in part, and we prophesy only in part; but when the complete comes, the partial will come to an end. When I was a child, I spoke like a child, I thought like a child, I reasoned like a child; when I became an adult, I put an end to childish ways. For now we see in a mirror, dimly, but then we will see face to face. Now I know only in part; then I will know fully, even as I have been fully known. And now faith, hope, and love abide, these three; and the greatest of these is love.

The Word of the Lord.

Without Love I Am Nothing

We told someone once about a wedding in which the readings had not included this passage and they said, half joking and half serious, "You mean you don't have to have this reading when you get married?" No, you don't *have* to have this reading—but it is as good a summary as you will ever find of the power and wonder of love! And even if you have heard it read at every wedding you ever attended, there is always more to be learned from it.

If you are thinking of using this reading, you might want to think about these things:

First, that God is hidden in it. The passage never refers to God. Some people may choose it for that reason: they are embarrassed to talk about God very much so they find it easier to talk vaguely about "love." But the Bible also says, "God is love." You can't talk about love without talking about God and you can't experience true love without experiencing God. One of the great gifts of love and marriage is the deeper experience we gain of the power of love—which is the power of God.

Second, that this passage is *not* talking about *your* love. It cannot be said of human love that it "bears all things, believes all things, hopes all things, endures all things." We might wish it were true, but it isn't. If we want to give or find that kind of love we need to look to God, not to ourselves or to each other. And it's good to know that. It takes a lot of the pressure off our marriages to know that we can find in God what we can't find in each other or in ourselves.

God is not mentioned here, but God is the subject of this passage. A marriage built on God's love has a security no human love can provide.

New Testament Reading 2

A Reading from the Letter of St. Paul to the Ephesians. [5:1-2, 21-33]

Therefore be imitators of God, as beloved children, and live in love, as Christ loved us and gave himself up for us, a fragrant offering and sacrifice to God. Be subject to one another out of reverence for Christ. Wives, be subject to your husbands as you are to the Lord. For the husband is the head of the wife just as Christ is the head of the church, the body of which he is the Savior. Just as the church is subject to Christ, so also wives ought to be, in everything, to their husbands. Husbands, love your wives, just as Christ loved the church and gave himself up for her, in order to make her holy by cleansing her with the washing of water by the word, so as to present the church to himself in splendor, without a spot or wrinkle or anything of the kind—yes, so that she may be holy and without blemish. In the same way, husbands should love their wives as they do their own bodies. He who loves his wife loves himself. For no one ever hates his own body, but he nourishes and tenderly cares for it, just as Christ does for the church, because we are members of his body. "For this reason a man will leave his father and mother and be joined to his wife, and the two will become one flesh." This is a great mystery, and I am applying it to Christ and the church. Each of you, however, should love his wife as himself, and a wife should respect her husband.

The Word of the Lord.

CHOICES for the Marriage Service of:

Bride _____

    Telephone: (H)_____ (O)_____

Groom _____

    Telephone: (H)_____ (O)_____

Date_____ Time_____ Place_____

Rehearsal date _____ Time _____

Presiding priest_____

    Telephone_____

Assisting priest or minister_____

    Telephone_____

Number expected at the wedding_____

Number of attendants:

    Ushers_____ Bridesmaids_____ Other_____

Bride's witness_____

Groom's witness_____

Service program to be printed: ☐ yes ☐ no

    By whom?_____

    to include: ☐ page references to Prayer Book
                  ☐ full text of service

                  ☐ hymn numbers, first lines
                  ☐ full text of hymns

                  ☐ references for readings, psalms
                  ☐ full texts

                  ☐ other_____

A

A. SERVICE

☐ Eucharist   ☐ Marriage service only

B. MUSIC

Organist _____

Telephone_____

Conference appointment: Date_____ Time_____

1. Prelude choices _____

   _____

   _____

   _____

   _____

   _____

2. Entrance music (bride's party)_____

   Entrance music (groom's party) _____

   Procession out _____

3. Hymns: 1)# _____ First line _____

   2)# _____ First line _____

   3)# _____ First line _____

   4)# _____ First line _____

4. Soloist(s) or instrumentalist(s)_____

   Music_____

   _____

C. THE ENTRANCE

☐ Bridal procession only

☐ Bride and groom process

☐ Informal entrance

B

D. THE PRESENTATION

1. ☐ Bride's escort "gives" the bride

2. ☐ Bride's escort "presents" the bride:

   a) ☐ "I"   b) ☐ "Her mother and I"

3. a) ☐ Bride's escort presents both

   b) ☐ Both escorts present bride and groom simultaneously

   c) ☐ Escorts present bride and groom separately

4. ☐ No formal presentation

E. THE MINISTRY OF THE WORD

First reading_____ Reader _____

Psalm_____ Leader _____ or Hymn _____

Second reading_____ Reader _____

Psalm_____ Leader _____ or Hymn _____

Gospel reading _____ Reader _____

The Apostles' Creed: ☐ yes ☐ no   The Nicene Creed: ☐ yes ☐ no

F. THE MARRIAGE

1. Procession to the altar?_____ music?_____

2. Vows: ☐ repeated ☐ memorized ☐ read

3. Rings: ☐ two   ☐ one   ☐ other gifts _____

   _____

   _____

G. THE PRAYERS

Lord's Prayer: ☐ old version   ☐ new version

Intercession: read by_____

Changes _____

H. THE BLESSING OF THE MARRIAGE

☐ Prayer 1 (p. 430)　　☐ Prayer 2 (p. 431)

I.　THE PEACE

☐ Omit

☐ Exchanged with wedding party　　☐ with congregation

J.　THE OFFERTORY

Bread and wine to be offered by couple?_____

Brought from_____

K. THE EUCHARISTIC PRAYER

☐ Prayer A　　☐ Prayer B　　☐ Prayer C　　☐ Prayer D

(If using Prayer D: Name(s) to be remembered: _____

_____)

L. THE COMMUNION

☐ All baptized persons　　☐ wedding party only

M.　THE DISMISSAL

☐ "Let us go forth in the Name of Christ"

☐ "Go in peace to love and serve the Lord"

☐ "Let us go forth . . . in the power of the Spirit"

☐ "Let us bless the Lord"

Live in Love

This passage is seldom read any more at weddings because it seems to put husbands in charge and wives in subjection. In fact, this passage revolutionized the way human beings looked at marriage and gave the woman's role a dignity it had never had before.

It's true that this passage was written two thousand years ago and what people needed to hear was quite different. Husbands needed to be told to love their wives as much as Christ loved the church and to be willing to sacrifice themselves for their wives as Christ died for the church. Wives, Saint Paul needed to teach the men of that day, are not mere property; wives are worth dying for. Perhaps today both husband and wife need to be reminded of that measure of love.

The passage also says that the wife should be "subject" to her husband but it begins by saying that all Christians should be "subject to one another." Today both husband and wife also need to hear that. People today give up on marriage because they aren't "getting anything out of it." But that's not what love is about. Love is about giving, not getting. And the example of love is Christ who gave himself completely for us.

So the lessons this passage gave to a first-century world are still vitally important, but may need to be applied even more broadly. Husbands *and* wives need to be subject to each other and give themselves for each other. Then the purpose for which God made us would be fulfilled and we would truly become "one flesh."

New Testament Reading 3

**A Reading from the Letter of St. Paul
to the Colossians.** [3:12-17]

As God's chosen ones, holy and beloved, clothe yourselves with compassion, kindness, humility, meekness, and patience. Bear with one another and, if anyone has a complaint against another, forgive each other; just as the Lord has forgiven you, so you also must forgive. Above all, clothe yourselves with love, which binds every thing together in perfect harmony. And let the peace of Christ rule in your hearts, to which indeed you were called in the one body. And be thankful. Let the word of Christ dwell in you richly; teach and admonish one another in all wisdom; and with gratitude in your hearts sing psalms, hymns, and spiritual songs to God. And whatever you do, in word or deed, do everything in the name of the Lord Jesus, giving thanks to God the Father through him.

The Word of the Lord.

Clothe Yourselves with Love

Anyone invited to a wedding spends a lot of time deciding what clothes to wear—and no one spends more time on that subject than the bride and groom. But this reading suggests that we also need to clothe ourselves with love. Well-chosen clothes can make us look very impressive for a few hours, but love makes a lasting difference.

How do you put on love? Perhaps sometimes we put on an appearance of love the way we put clothes on and take them off, but real love comes from God and enters the heart. When we clothe ourselves with love we appear different because we really are different, because love is at the center of our lives.

All the other virtues mentioned—compassion, patience, kindness, and so on—come from love. But none of them is automatic. Saint Paul has advice on how to acquire them. We need, he says, to center our thoughts on God's love for us by hearing God's word and singing God's praise. Then, if everything we do is done "in the Name of the Lord Jesus, giving thanks to God . . . through him," love will be not only our clothing but also our food and the whole of our being.

New Testament Reading 4

A Reading from the First Letter of St. John.
[4:7-16]

Beloved, let us love one another, because love is from God; everyone who loves is born of God and knows God. Whoever does not love does not know God, for God is love. God's love was revealed among us in this way: God sent his only Son into the world so that we might live through him. In this is love, not that we loved God but that he loved us and sent his Son to be the atoning sacrifice for our sins. Beloved, since God loved us so much, we also ought to love one another. No one has ever seen God; if we love one another, God lives in us, and his love is perfected in us. By this we know that we abide in him and he in us, because he has given us of his Spirit. And we have seen and do testify that the Father has sent his Son as the Savior of the world. God abides in those who confess that Jesus is the Son of God, and they abide in God. So we have known and believe the love that God has for us. God is love, and those who abide in love abide in God, and God abides in them.

The Word of the Lord.

God is Love

The simplest definition of God ever given is provided in this First Letter of Saint John in three one-syllable words: "God is love." Therefore, says the author, "those who abide in love abide in God." If you are filled with love, you are filled with God. It is God who gives you your love for each other, and in knowing that love you come to know God.

But this equation cannot be reversed. "God is love," but love is not God. The danger of being in love is that we can be so wrapped up in ourselves and each other that we stop there. We make our love for each other the meaning of life. And it isn't. Some people are satisfied to find a few nuggets of gold in the gravel banks of the stream and never move upstream to find the source of the gold. If you think your love for each other is wonderful, imagine what God's love must be like!

Notice how logical Saint John is: "If God loved us so much, we also ought to love one another." If someone gave us so great a gift, we also ought to give gifts. When we realize that our love for each other is a gift we could never earn, we may respond by trying to love others and especially those who have least earned or deserved it. Only when love is so freely shared will the world be the place of love and peace God intended it to be.

New Testament Reading 5

A Reading from the Revelation to St. John.
[19:6-9]

Then I heard what seemed to be the voice of a great multitude, like the sound of many waters and like the sound of mighty thunderpeals, crying out, "Hallelujah! For the Lord our God the Almighty reigns. Let us rejoice and exult and give him the glory, for the marriage of the Lamb has come, and his bride has made herself ready; to her it has been granted to be clothed with fine linen, bright and pure"— for the fine linen is the righteous deeds of the saints. And the angel said to me, "Write this: Blessed are those who are invited to the marriage supper of the Lamb." And he said to me, "These are true words of God."

The Word of the Lord.

Invited to the Marriage Supper of the Lamb

Several of the suggested readings for marriage compare heaven itself to a marriage feast. And that means that a marriage feast can be a foretaste of heaven. A marriage feast is a time of joy, it unites many people in the happiness of others, and it is centered on love: all those are true of heaven—only more so! If the readings at your wedding remind people of the greater joy and greater love which God promises, that could be a gift of love for you to give them.

The marriage in this vision of heaven is the marriage of Jesus ("the Lamb") and the church ("his bride"). The opening statement in the marriage service also tells us that marriage "signifies to us the mystery of the union between Christ and his Church," so this passage picks up the same theme and helps explain it. You might also remember the hymn, "The church's one foundation," which says of Jesus

from heaven he came and sought her to be his holy bride, with his own blood he bought her and for her life he died.

So the unity we have with each other in marriage is like the unity God wants to have with us. We can learn something of the depth and power of God's love by experiencing the depth and power of the unity between a husband and wife.

Gospel Reading 1

**The Holy Gospel of Our Lord Jesus Christ
according to St. Matthew.**   [5:1-10]

When Jesus saw the crowds, he went up the mountain; and after he sat down, his disciples came to him. Then he began to speak, and taught them, saying: "Blessed are the poor in spirit, for theirs is the kingdom of heaven. Blessed are those who mourn, for they will be comforted. Blessed are the meek, for they will inherit the earth. Blessed are those who hunger and thirst for righteousness, for they will be filled. Blessed are the merciful, for they will receive mercy. Blessed are the pure in heart, for they will see God. Blessed are the peacemakers, for they will be called children of God. Blessed are those who are persecuted for righteousness' sake, for theirs is the kingdom of heaven."

The Gospel of the Lord.

A Reversal of Values

Some modern translations of this passage use the word "happy" instead of "blessed." We may think of "blessedness" as God's gift and "happiness" as more self-centered, but true happiness is God's gift.

Notice that Jesus says that the ones who are blessed or happy are those who are poor and hungry and persecuted. When he says, "Blessed are those who mourn," it almost seems like a contradiction in terms. How can you be happy when you are unhappy? But those who have lost everything in this world's terms are most open to God's presence. As long as we are rich and contented we are less likely to seek God, yet without God we cannot be truly happy.

Love and marriage make us aware that happiness comes from another. But even that human other (though we may think otherwise when we are first engaged and first married!) cannot satisfy all our needs. Finally, we still need God.

The world around us talks about "self-fulfillment" and "self-realization." The world around us uses other people for selfish ends. But real love teaches us to look outside ourselves for happiness. Real love is ready to sacrifice self for the other. We empty ourselves—and are filled with love from outside ourselves. We have to learn to reverse the world's values to understand what true happiness is.

Gospel Reading 2

**The Holy Gospel of Our Lord Jesus Christ
according to St. Matthew.**   [22:1-14]

Once more Jesus spoke to them in parables, say-ing: "The kingdom of heaven may be compared to a king who gave a wedding banquet for his son. He sent his slaves to call those who had been invited to the wedding banquet, but they would not come. Again he sent other slaves, saying, 'Tell those who have been invited: Look, I have prepared my dinner, my oxen and my fat calves have been slaughtered, and everything is ready; come to the wedding ban-quet.' But they made light of it and went away, one to his farm, another to his business, while the rest seized his slaves, mistreated them, and killed them. The king was enraged. He sent his troops, destroyed those murderers, and burned their city. Then he said to his slaves, 'The wedding is ready, but those invited were not worthy. Go therefore into the main streets, and invite everyone you find to the wedding banquet.' Those slaves went out into the streets and gathered all whom they found, both good and bad; so the wedding hall was filled with guests. But when the king came in to see the guests, he noticed a man there who was not wearing a wedding robe, and he said to him, 'Friend, how did you get in here without a wedding robe?' And he was speechless. Then the king said to the attendants, 'Bind him hand and foot, and throw him into the outer dark-ness, where there will be weeping and gnashing of teeth.' For many are called, but few are chosen."

The Gospel of the Lord.

✝

Preparing for Marriage

The violence in this passage makes it a rather unusual choice for a reading at a wedding service—but it would get people's attention! Here are some points you might think about in considering this passage:

1) The Bible compares heaven to a wedding feast (mentioned in a number of the other choices of readings). God calls us into the kingdom of heaven in order to fill us with love and joy as the king does in this story—and we had better get ready! If our friends truly care about us, they will knock themselves out to get to our wedding. If we truly care for God, we will make the same effort to respond to God's invitation.

2) A wedding involves not just two people but many. It takes the cooperation of many people and an enormous amount of planning. As you plan your wedding you will discover this; perhaps you already have! And this is what makes marriage like God's kingdom. Some people think of religion as a "private" or a "personal" matter. But the word "religion" comes from a word that means "to bind together." Faith binds together not only our own life but all life. The biblical vision is a vision of faith calling people together and uniting them in joy. There's no room in that vision for the person who doesn't respond to the invitation or who comes without making any effort to look presentable. People are sometimes shocked to think that God would act like the king in this story, but how would you react if people threw away your invitation or came to your wedding in dirty clothes? Would you find it easy still to consider them your friends? God is very forgiving, but God can hardly force us to enjoy the feast if we simply ignore the invitation.

Think about this reading carefully before choosing it and ask the priest if she or he would want to do a homily on it. It might be a way to help people understand what it means to live in God's world and be called to take part in the joy of the kingdom of God.

Gospel Reading 3

The Holy Gospel of our Lord Jesus Christ according to St. Mark. [10:6-9, 13-16]

Jesus said, "But from the beginning of creation, 'God made them male and female.' 'For this reason a man shall leave his father and mother and be joined to his wife, and the two shall become one flesh.' So they are no longer two, but one flesh. Therefore what God has joined together, let no one separate." People were bringing little children to him in order that he might touch them; and the disciples spoke sternly to them. But when Jesus saw this, he was indignant and said to them, "Let the little children come to me; do not stop them; for it is to such as these that the kingdom of God belongs. Truly I tell you, whoever does not receive the kingdom of God as a little child will never enter it." And he took them up in his arms, laid his hands on them, and blessed them.

The Gospel of the Lord.

As a Little Child

One clear dividing line between childhood and adulthood is marriage. Parents may finally be forced to recognize that their children have really grown up and gone when they get married. Yet this reading talks about becoming child-like.

The fact is, however, that when it comes to experience in marriage, newlyweds are really "children," really beginners. It takes a lot of living together to develop a mature, grown-up relationship. And it's good to be reminded of that. Children are allowed to make mistakes. No one expects them to have all the answers. Nor should you expect yourself or your partner to have all the answers. So allow yourselves to be children, to make mistakes, and keep on growing.

And children are eager to learn—as a married couple should be. Children are also trusting—as married people should be. And children enjoy life—as newlyweds certainly ought to. Jesus said we should be like children to enter the kingdom. So you don't need always to be sober and wise adults—at least not for a while.

This reading also is the one place in which Jesus spoke directly about the meaning of marriage. He said that God deliberately created the human race male and female so that the two would come together and be "one flesh." That, too, takes a lot of living, but it's wonderful when it really happens. In fact, marriage is a kind of school in which we learn to be what God wants the whole human race to be: a united body of people who love each other because they know God's love for them.

Gospel Reading 4

The Holy Gospel of Our Lord Jesus Christ
according to St. Luke.   [24:13-35]

Now on that same day two of them were going to a village called Emmaus, about seven miles from Jerusalem, and talking with each other about all these things that had happened. While they were talking and discussing, Jesus himself came near and went with them, but their eyes were kept from recognizing him. And he said to them, "What are you discussing with each other while you walk along?" They stood still, looking sad. Then one of them, whose name was Cleopas, answered him, "Are you the only stranger in Jerusalem who does not know the things that have taken place there in these days?" He asked them, "What things?" They replied, "The things about Jesus of Nazareth, who was a prophet mighty in deed and word before God and all the people, and how our chief priests and leaders handed him over to be condemned to death and crucified him. But we had hoped that he was the one to redeem Israel. Yes, and besides all this, it is now the third day since these things took place. Moreover, some women of our group astounded us. They were at the tomb early this morning, and when they did not find his body there, they came back and told us that they had indeed seen a vision of angels who said that he was alive. Some of those who were with us went to the tomb and found it just as the women had said; but they did not see him."

Then he said to them, "Oh, how foolish you are, and how slow of heart to believe all that the prophets have declared! Was it not necessary that the Messiah should suffer these things and then enter into his glory?" Then beginning with Moses and all the prophets, he interpreted to them the things about himself in all the scriptures. As they came near the village to which they were going, he walked ahead as if he were going on. But they urged him strongly, saying, "Stay with us, because it is almost evening and the day is now nearly over." So he went in to stay with them. When he was at the table with them, he took bread, blessed and broke it, and gave it to them. Then their eyes were opened, and they recognized him; and he vanished from their sight. They said to each other, "Were not our hearts burning within us while he was talking to us on the road, while he was opening the scriptures to us?" That same hour they got up and returned to Jerusalem; and they found the eleven and their companions gathered together. They were saying, "The Lord has risen indeed, and he has appeared to Simon!" Then they told what had happened on the road, and how he had been made known to them in the breaking of the bread.

The Gospel of the Lord.

Made Known in the Breaking of the Bread

This is a long passage but it tells a wonderful story. It is not a story about marriage directly, but it is a story about two disciples (perhaps a husband and wife) who walked with Jesus without recognizing him until he "did something religious." Isn't that often the way life is? We walk together and talk together and get engaged and get married and still may not really understand that God has been walking with us the whole time. Afterwards we may remember that "our hearts (were) burning within us," but at the time we thought it was our own happiness, not God's gift.

This is also a story about the importance of food as a symbol. Have you ever stopped to think what an obvious symbol the sharing of bread is? Sharing food is always a sign of love. We do it in our families, and it is not only a way of expressing love but also a way of building love. What would happen to a family that never sat down together at a meal? (Remember this when you find yourselves dashing out of the house with a roll in one hand, eating lunch at your desk, and getting home after everyone else has eaten. A family can't survive a schedule like that for long!) Eating together draws us closer. And sharing food with the hungry also draws us closer to those in need. Sharing food builds love in a world that needs more love.

And this is a story about the eucharist and how week by week God is "made known to (us) in the breaking of the bread." A marriage that begins at God's altar and continues to come back to God's altar will be a marriage constantly strengthened by God's presence, God's strength, and God's joy.

Gospel Reading 5

***The Holy Gospel of Our Lord Jesus Christ
according to St. John.***   [2:1-11]

On the third day there was a wedding in Cana
of Galilee, and the mother of Jesus was there.
Jesus and his disciples had also been invited to
the wedding. When the wine gave out, the mother
of Jesus said to him, "They have no wine." And
Jesus said to her, "Woman, what concern is that
to you and to me? My hour has not yet come."
His mother said to the servants, "Do whatever he
tells you." Now standing there were six stone
water jars for the Jewish rites of purification,
each holding twenty or thirty gallons. Jesus said
to them, "Fill the jars with water." And they filled
them up to the brim. He said to them, "Now draw
some out, and take it to the chief steward." So
they took it. When the steward tasted the water
that had become wine, and did not know where it
came from (though the servants who had drawn
the water knew), the steward called the bride-
groom and said to him, "Everyone serves the
good wine first, and then the inferior wine after
the guests have become drunk. But you have kept
the good wine until now." Jesus did this, the first
of his signs, in Cana of Galilee, and revealed his
glory; and his disciples believed in him.

The Gospel of the Lord.

✝

A Wedding in Cana

For many centuries this was the only gospel ever read at a Christian wedding. If you like tradition, that alone may be a reason to choose this passage! But there are lots of other reasons for this choice.

First of all, this passage tells about Jesus at a wedding feast: not just at the service, but at the celebration afterwards. That's a useful starting place. It's easy to remember God's presence during the church service, but not so easy to remember God's presence at the reception and wedding dinner. Yet Jesus is there, as he was at the wedding in Cana, not center stage (that's your place), but sitting on the side and ready to give help as needed. Very few people in Cana ever realized what had happened or how close they came to running out of supplies for the party. The fact that we don't notice God's presence, doesn't mean God isn't there.

Second, this reading makes connections between the wedding party, the other meals we will share, and the eucharist. Every meal, all sharing of food, is a religious act. Families are drawn together at meals as at no other time, and the great moments of our lives—holidays like Thanksgiving and Christmas and Easter, birthdays and weddings and even funerals—bring us together around a table. But the sharing of food with the hungry is also an act of faith—faith that God will continue to give to us as we give to others, and faith that what God gives to us is meant to be shared.

Third, there is a message here about God's power. God can take mere water and transform it into the best wine. God can take mere bread and wine and make them vehicles of God's presence.

And fourth (but not last; there's much more to be learned from this passage!), remember that God often saves the best until last. You may think when you become engaged or when you are married, that nothing better can happen. In fact, this is only a beginning. God always has more to give: the best things seldom come first and are always worth waiting for.

Gospel Reading 6

**The Holy Gospel of Our Lord Jesus Christ
according to St. John.** [15:9-16]

Jesus said, "As the Father has loved me, so I have loved you; abide in my love. If you keep my commandments, you will abide in my love, just as I have kept my Father's commandments and abide in his love. I have said these things to you so that my joy may be in you, and that your joy may be complete. "This is my commandment, that you love one another as I have loved you. No one has greater love than this, to lay down one's life for one's friends. You are my friends if you do what I command you. I do not call you servants any longer, because the servant does not know what the master is doing; but I have called you friends, because I have made known to you everything that I have heard from my Father. You did not choose me but I chose you. And I appointed you to go and bear fruit, fruit that will last, so that the Father will give you whatever you ask him in my name."

The Gospel of the Lord.

✝

A Command, a Choice, a Result

There's so much to think about in this passage that the main problem may be choosing one theme on which to concentrate.

Notice first that these are Jesus' words to his disciples at the Last Supper. Here again, it is at a meal that we learn to love. Remember also that it was at the Last Supper that Jesus gave another command: "Do this in remembrance of me." So it is at a meal that we are commanded to love and to remember Jesus' presence in our lives.

It may seem odd that we are *commanded* to love. We usually think that love is a matter of feelings and that we can't be told to love. But the fact is that the primary difference between being married and just living together is that we accept a command to love. Those who simply live together are free to leave at any time; those who are married are not. So why should we accept such limits on our freedom? Because our emotions aren't always there for us when we need them. There will be days when we don't feel very loving, but the command to love, the fact that we are married, keeps our relationship in place anyway.

"I chose you," Jesus said. We usually think of this as meaning his choice of the apostles, but it applies to us also. We are Christians not just because of our upbringing or even our own decision, but because God chose us and called us. God can work in our lives in many ways and without our being aware. But God chose us not only to know God's love and respond to that love, but also to know human love and to be married to each other. We think we choose to marry each other but, at a deeper level, God chose you for each other as a means of showing you how great God's love can be.

And you are commanded to "bear fruit." All love has results. In a marriage the result of love may be children. But the fruit of a marriage should never be limited to children. The love of a married couple for each other should lead to greater love for other human beings and to a world in which we are more likely to reach out to those in need. The fruit of love should be a world of justice and peace.

Supplemental Reading 1

A Reading from Saint Augustine.

"Sing to the Lord a new song; his praise is in the assembly of the saints." We are urged to sing a new song to the Lord, as singers who have learned a new song. A song is a thing of joy; more profoundly, it is a thing of love. Anyone, therefore, who has learned to love the new life has learned to sing a new song, and the new song reminds us of our new life. The new singer, the new song, the new covenant, all belong to the one kingdom of God, and so the new singer will sing a new song and will belong to the new covenant.

We cannot love unless someone has loved us first. The source of our love for God can only be found in the fact that God loved us first. This love is not something we generate ourselves; it comes to us through the Holy Spirit who has been given to us.

Now it is your unquestioned desire to sing of him whom you love, but you ask me how to sing his praises. You have heard the words: "Sing to the Lord a new song," and you wish to know what praises to sing. The answer is: "His praise is in the assembly of the saints"; it is in the singers themselves. If you desire to praise him, then live what you express. Live good lives, and you yourselves will be his praise.

Here ends the Reading.

Sing Praise with your Lives

"We cannot love," writes Saint Augustine, "unless someone has loved us first." Those who fall in love know that love comes from outside and creates an answering love within us. The person with whom we fall in love creates a response in us. But the love that is awakened in us by that other special person doesn't begin with them. They will be the first to tell you that the love between you didn't begin in them. They probably think it began with you!

But the fact is that the love we "find" in another has a source outside both, and that source is God. God creates the love we feel. It's important to recognize that because then we will know where to turn when our own love fails. Some people blame it on themselves and some blame it on the other. But God is the source and we need to turn to God for the constant renewal of our love.

Saint Augustine, who died in the year 431 A.D., was one of the first truly great Christian theologians and his work is still studied. He lived in a time of social chaos and enormous change and he realized that we cannot look for perfection or stability or examples on earth; we need to look for them in heaven. But the love of heaven must be seen in human lives. Therefore we must constantly renew our love by turning to God and we must let God's love be reflected in our lives.

Supplemental Reading 2

A *Reading from* Revelations of Divine Love *by Julian of Norwich*

Our Lord showed me a little thing, the size of a hazelnut, in the palm of my hand; and it was as round as a ball. I looked thereupon with the eye of my understanding, and thought, "What may this be?" And it was generally answered thus, "It is all that is made." I marvelled how it might last, for I thought it might suddenly have fallen to nothing for littleness. And I was answered in my understanding, "It lasts, and ever shall last, because God loves it. And so all things have their being by the love of God."

And from that time that it was showed, I desired often to know what was our Lord's meaning. And I was answered in spiritual understanding, "Would you understand your Lord's meaning? Understand it well: Love was God's meaning. Who showed it to you? Love. What did he show you? Love. Why did God show it to you? For love." Thus did I learn that Love was our Lord's meaning.

And I saw full surely in this and in all, that ere God made us God loved us; which love was never slackened nor ever shall be. And in this love God has done all that God made; and in this love God has made all things profitable to us; and in this love our life is everlasting. In our making we had beginning; for the love wherein God made us was in God from without beginning; in which love we have our beginning. And all this shall we see in God, without end. Which may Jesus grant us.

Here ends the Reading.

Love is our Beginning

Marriage is probably the closest most of us ever come to making a really complete new **beginning** in our lives. We choose to make a total change: to give up our "independence" and join ourselves with another human being for the rest of our life. And we do it because of love.

Julian of Norwich was a wonderful woman who lived in the fourteenth century and had visions of God and wrote down what she saw and heard. She saw that all of life is like a tiny hazelnut in God's hand: God holds our lives in love. She saw that love comes from God and that we come from God and that the love we experience comes from God. So everything begins with God's love.

Remember, then, that you did have another beginning—when you were born. And that beginning also was the result of love: your parent's love for each other. You had your beginning in their love. And now you will have a new beginning in the love God has given you for each other.

And your love also is a beginning, a source of love that will flow out to others: to children, to friends, to those with whom you work. Your love is part of the process by which God is beginning to re-create the world.

Remember also that in the love of God you can always begin again. However badly we may fail each other, God's love brings forgiveness. And with God's forgiveness, we also can forgive and find a new beginning of love.

Supplemental Reading 3

A Reading from John Donne.

The first marriage that was made, God made, and he made it in Paradise. The last marriage which shall be made, God shall make too, and in Paradise too; in the Kingdom of heaven: and at that marriage, I hope in him that shall make it, to meet, not some, but all this company. From all eternity in the Book of Life, in God's eternal Decree for my election, there Christ was married to my soul. Before my soul was a soul, did Christ marry my soul in his eternal Decree. So it was eternal, it had no beginning. Neither doth he interrupt this by giving me any occasion of jealousy by the way, but loves my soul as though there were no other soul, and would have done and suffered all that he did for me alone, if there had been no name but mine in the Book of life. And he hath married me to him, *in aeturnum*, for ever, before all beginnings, and *in aeturnum*, for ever, without any interruptions, so I know that *whom he loves he loves to the end*, and that he hath given me, not a presumptuous impossibility, but a modest infallibility that no sin of mine shall divorce or separate me from him. There where the Angels, which cannot die could not live, this very body which cannot choose but die, shall live, and live as long as that God of life that made it.

Here ends the Reading.

The First Marriage and the Last

Perhaps because they are brought up on stories of pioneers in the wilderness, Americans often have the feeling that whatever they do, they are doing something new, that no one ever did before. Perhaps everyone feels that way about getting married. It is all so new to us and so wonderful that we can believe (and tell each other) that "no two people have ever been so in love" and that our marriage is totally different and new.

John Donne, one of the greatest of English poets and Dean of St. Paul's Cathedral in the seventeenth century, says in this marriage sermon that every marriage is a part of God's purpose which began with the Creation of the world and will end in the kingdom of God. God's purpose, says Donne, has always been and always will be to marry us, to bring human beings together in love. God began to do it in Paradise and God will complete the work in heaven. Your marriage is a part of God's eternal purpose and a part of the plan by which God is preparing us for eternal life.

To put it another way, God has been marrying people for a long time. Your love for each other is, indeed, from one point of view, brand new and very wonderful. But marriage itself is not new. There are many marriages both good and bad and we can learn from them all. More important, God's greater plan is to marry us, to draw all humanity together in love. We are supported and sustained and strengthened by this cosmic ocean of love within which we live and through which God is drawing us into that final and perfect marriage feast in the kingdom of heaven.

Supplemental Reading 4

A Reading from **Waiting on God** *by Simone Weil.*

Before all things, God is love. Before all things, God loves himself. This love, this friendship of God, is the Trinity. Between the terms united by this relation of divine love there is more than nearness; there is infinite nearness or identity. But, resulting from the Creation, the Incarnation and the Passion, there is also infinite distance. The totality of space and the totality of time, interposing their immensity, put an infinite distance between God and God.

Lovers or friends desire two things. The one is to love each other so much that they enter into each other and only make one being. The other is to love each other so much that, having half the globe between them, their union will not be diminished in the slightest degree. All any human being desires here below is perfectly realized in God. We have all these impossible desires within us as a mark of our destination.

The love between God and God, which in itself *is* God, is this bond of double virtue; the bond which unites two beings so closely that they are no longer distinguishable and really form a single unity, and the bond which stretches across distance and triumphs over infinite separation.

It is only necessary to know that love is a direction and not a state of the soul.

Here ends the Reading.

Distance and Identity

Being in love makes us aware as never before of nearness and separation. Perhaps we learn how we can be holding someone else tightly and yet not sure where they are. We can also be distant from someone and yet completely identified with them. Love unites us with another person across any distance, yet leaves us still wanting to be closer and more deeply united.

Simone Weil was a French woman of Jewish ancestry who wanted to identify herself with the needs of others. She was a teacher of philosophy who worked in a car factory and on farms and experienced the horrors of war during the Spanish Civil War. Although she was in England during World War II working for the French Government in Exile, she refused to eat anything more than her compatriots in France were allowed and died in 1943 at the age of 34 as a result of her self-sacrifice. Although she was deeply attracted to Christian thought, she never became a Christian since she felt that God was not calling her to be baptized and that she must be "waiting on God." Perhaps that same mystery of distance and identity was at work in that decision.

In another place, Simone Weil speaks of how God went the distance of the universe to be united with us and how that separation of God from God is represented in the cross. Love suffers for the sake of love. But love can overcome infinite division.

Supplemental Reading 5

A Reading from **The Hymn of the Universe**
by Teilhard de Chardin.

Only love can bring individual beings to their perfect completion, as individuals, by uniting them one with another, because only love takes possession of them and unites them by what lies deepest within them. This is simply a fact of our everyday experience. For indeed at what moment do lovers come into the most complete possession of themselves if not when they say that they are lost in one another? And is not love all the time achieving—in couples, in teams, all around us—the magical and reputedly contradictory feat of personalizing through totalizing? And why should not what is thus daily achieved on a small scale be repeated one day on world-wide dimensions?

Humanity, the spirit of the earth, the synthesis of individuals and peoples, the paradoxical conciliation of the element with the whole, of the one with the many: all these are regarded as utopian fantasies, yet they are biologically necessary; and if we would see them made flesh in the world what more need we do than imagine our power to love growing and broadening till it can embrace the totality of human beings and of the earth?

Here ends the Reading.

Only Love Can Bring Completion

Some people, when they fall in love, imagine that the universe revolves around them. Teilhard de Chardin, a Jesuit paleontologist of the twentieth century, would tend to agree. He was a scientist who studied dinosaur bones in the Gobi desert, but he came to believe that the whole creation was evolving toward a single purpose, an "Omega point" in which all will be united in love. The love you feel for each other is, then, truly a part of God's universal purpose and needs room to grow until it takes in the whole of creation.

That understanding of love, however, can result either in silly songs about having "the world on a string" or in the kind of self-sacrifice that inspired the greatest saints. A love that shapes the universe is not going to make our lives simple. If God's purpose in us is to unite the universe in love, then that purpose is challenged by ethnic tensions, petty rivalries at the office, hunger and homelessness in our communities, and the days when our partner seems to forget that we are even alive.

Can we believe in a universe evolving toward unity and love when we read the newspapers? Only if love remains strong at the center of our own lives and only if we constantly turn toward God to renew the love we know now. God's purpose depends on God, not on us. But if we turn to God in worship and prayer, the power of the love at work in our lives can indeed be a part of the working out of God's purpose.

Supplemental Reading 6

A *Reading from* The Strength to Love
by Martin Luther King, Jr.

The meaning of love is not to be confused with some sentimental outpouring. Love is something much more than emotional bosh. An overflowing love which seeks nothing in return, is the love of God operating in the human heart. Love is the most durable power in the world . . . the most potent instrument available in mankind's quest for peace and security. The great military leaders of the past have gone, and their empires have crumbled and burned to ashes. But the empire of Jesus, built solidly and majestically on the foundation of love, is still growing.

Here ends the Reading.

Creating a New World

The love that brings us to be married is usually felt as a very personal thing, a powerful bond between two human beings. Two people fall in love and the rest of the world can seem to be completely irrelevant. Who cares about those people out there? We have us!

But love is bigger than that. You can't plan a wedding without realizing how many people are involved in your love. There are many people you love and who love you and many of them will be there when you get married.

But love is also bigger than that. Notice how the prayers in the marriage service (pp. 429-430) speak about a love which will "reach out in love and concern for others." This is the love Martin Luther King, Jr., preached and practiced, a powerful love which transformed the pattern of American life. Love broke down age-old barriers and brought people together who had been bitterly divided. Love can, indeed, change the world.

In the midst of your personal happiness and your love for each other, it may be important to remember that your love is part of the power by which God is creating a whole new world.

Supplemental Reading 7

A Reading from **The Irrational Season**
by Madeleine L'Engle

Ultimately there comes a time when a decision must be made. Ultimately two people who love each other must ask themselves how much they hope for as their love grows and deepens, and how much risk they are willing to take. It is indeed a fearful gamble. Because it is the nature of love to create, a marriage itself is something which has to be created.

To marry is the biggest risk in human relations that a person can take. If we commit ourselves to one person for life this is not, as many people think, a rejection of freedom; rather it demands the courage to move into all the risks of freedom, and the risk of love which is permanent; into that love which is not possession but participation. It takes a lifetime to learn another person.

When love is not possession, but participation, then it is part of that co-creation which is our human calling.

Here ends the Reading.

The Risk of Love

Lots of children have read books by Madeleine L'Engle, and every married couple could benefit by reading **Two-Part Invention**, which is the story of her own marriage. She writes about the risks of marriage from experience.

Marriage involves taking risks. How well do you really know each other? What qualifications do you have for parenting a child? Will you be able to deal gracefully with the loss of a job, with the mornings when you wake up feeling mad at the world, with sickness, with old age? You can't answer those questions ahead of time, but if you love each other and trust in God's loving help, you will take the risk.

And risk sometimes means failure. Someone has said that if you don't make four major mistakes before lunch, you aren't really trying. Risk involves failure, and failure leads to forgiveness—and forgiveness creates a deeper unity. "It is the nature of love to create." And love can create even out of failure. That's what makes the risk worth taking.

Supplemental Reading 8

A Reading from The Hungering Dark
by Frederick Buechner.

Dostoevski describes Alexei Karamazov falling asleep and dreaming about the wedding at Cana, and for him too it is a dream of indescribable joy, but when he wakes from it he does a curious thing. He throws himself down on the earth and embraces it. He kisses the earth and among tears that are in no way sentimental because they are turned not inward but outward he forgives the earth and begs its forgiveness and vows to love it forever. And that is the heart of it, after all, and matrimony is called holy because this brave and fateful promise of a man and a woman to love and honor and serve each other through thick and thin looks beyond itself to more fateful promises still and speaks mightily of what human life at its most human and most alive and most holy must always be.

A dream is a compression of time where the dreamer can live through a whole constellation of events in no more time than it takes a curtain to rustle in the room where he sleeps. In dreams time does not so much flow on as it flows up, like water from a deep spring. And in this way every wedding is a dream, and every word that is spoken there means more than it says, and every gesture—the clasping of hands, the giving of rings—is rich with mystery. Part of the mystery is that Christ is there as he was in Cana once, and the joy of a wedding, and maybe even sometimes the tears, are a miracle that he works. But when the wedding feast was over, he set his face toward Jerusalem and started out for the hour that had not yet come but was to come soon enough.

And so it was also, we hope, with the bride and groom at Cana and with every bride and groom—that the love they bear one another and the joy they take in one another may help them grow in love for this whole troubled world where their final joy lies.

Here ends the Reading.

The Wedding at Cana

One of the questions people have to ask today as they plan their wedding is, "Do we want to videotape it?" It's easy to arrange for someone to stand in a quiet corner and tape the service so that it can be seen again later on a television screen.

But most couples seem to prefer not to. Perhaps they know instinctively that the magic and mystery of the marriage can never be captured on film. Life can never be stopped and played back or "re-experienced." Marriage is "holy," it is part of a mysterious power through which God is at work in the world.

Frederick Buechner is a contemporary writer who says something about this in a wedding sermon. He points to the way marriage involves tears as well as joy, pain as well as happiness. He speaks of the way love always leads us further than we expected to go and makes us aware of the needs of others around us.

The joy and meaning of marriage can never stop at the church door or at the door of the home we create. The love we give each other rubs off on others. It helps us face the hard things in life. It changes the world we live in. It builds the kingdom of God.

October 2014

Dear Friends,

Like many others, I've always been fascinated with angels. My father saw an angel shortly before he died. The angel arrived in the middle of the night in human form, dressed in farm clothes, and helped my dad back to bed. Dad described the angel in detail. Angels among us isn't as far removed from reality as it might seem. Check out Hebrews 13:2 if you don't believe me. It was that verse that inspired *Mrs. Miracle* and now . . . drumroll, please . . . *Mr. Miracle.*

I owe a great deal to several people who made this entire project possible. First and foremost my agent, Theresa Park, and her incredible staff, Emily, Alex, Andrea, Abby, and Peter. And, of course, my two marvelous Ballantine editors, Jennifer Hershey and Shauna Summers, who encouraged and supported me through each phase of the writing process, along with my own amazing staff.

So now, my wonderful readers, it's your turn. I hope you enjoy the story of Harry Mills as he discovers the delights and pleasures of life on Earth along with its temptations and limitations. And then, of course, there's his mission with Addie and Erich . . . oh heavens (pun intended), there I go again. Okay, I won't say anything more. The story is for you to unfold by turning the page. I hope that you're charmed by *Mr. Miracle* and that you, too, might find an angel or two in your own life.

Your feedback is important to me. You can contact me through my webpage at DebbieMacomber.com or through Facebook. If you're so inclined you can write me at P.O. Box 1458, Port Orchard, WA 98366.

Merry Christmas and may God bless.

Debbie Macomber

For a complete list of books by Debbie Macomber,
visit her website at www.debbiemacomber.com.

Mr. Miracle

DEBBIE MACOMBER

Mr. Miracle

A Christmas Novel

BALLANTINE BOOKS

NEW YORK

Copyright © 2014 by Debbie Macomber
Excerpt from *Starry Night* by Debbie Macomber
copyright © 2013 by Debbie Macomber

All rights reserved.

Published in the United States by Ballantine Books, an imprint of Random House, a division of Random House LLC, a Penguin Random House Company, New York.

BALLANTINE and the HOUSE colophon are registered trademarks of Random House LLC.

LIBRARY OF CONGRESS CATALOGING-IN-PUBLICATION DATA
Macomber, Debbie.
Mr. Miracle : a Christmas novel / Debbie Macomber.
pages cm
ISBN 978-0-8041-7758-0
eBook ISBN 978-0-553-39162-6
1. Guardian angels—Fiction. 2. Women college students—Fiction.
3. Man-woman relationships—Fiction. 4. Christmas stories. I. Title.
PS3563.A2364M75 2014
813'.54—dc23   2014027142

Printed in the United States of America on acid-free paper

www.ballantinebooks.com

2 4 6 8 9 7 5 3 1

Special Walmart Edition

Book design by Dana Leigh Blanchette

To Bill Abbott
in appreciation for his confidence
and faith in me

and in memory of Tommy
who really was Man's Best Friend

Mr. Miracle

Prologue

Well, well, well, Harry Mills mused as he glanced around the campus of Southshore Community College. *So this is Earth.* Students darted across the emerald-green landscape, scurrying toward their classes. The December sky was dark and overcast, threatening rain. Not uncommon weather for the Pacific Northwest, or so he'd been told.

This is exactly what I expected, he thought a bit smugly. Until now he'd had, shall we say, a heavenly perspective. Yes, he was an angel, but unlike his fellow angels and good friends, Shirley, Goodness, and Mercy, he had the ability to mingle with humans without suspicion. What he enjoyed most was the fact that the humans were completely un-aware of who he was and the work he'd been given. Harry was on a God-given mission—a trial mission that was the opportunity of an eternity and one he hoped would become a permanent job if he performed well.

In preparation for his earthly visitation, Harry had carefully studied human behavior and had learned about ways to gently guide his charges. Of course, he knew all about free will, too, but frankly, he wasn't overly concerned. Just how difficult could it be to give a nudge to those in need of a bit of subtle direction? Naturally, he was required to work under certain parameters—restrictions, actually—but he didn't consider that a particular problem, either.

What did concern Harry was that he'd been assigned a mentor, which in his opinion was completely unnecessary. He didn't need anyone looking over his shoulder, watching his every move.

As the spiritual coordinator for this part of Tacoma, Celeste Chapeaux had been assigned to oversee Harry. Her powers were above and beyond his own. While his role involved the students in his class, her sphere of influence reached far beyond as coordinator of an entire area, including the campus and surrounding neighborhood. Harry knew he wasn't the only angel under her direction.

For now, Harry was willing to play by the rules in order to prove himself. In time, Celeste would realize an angel of his knowledge and intelligence was capable of managing assignments on his own without supervision.

Making his way across the campus, Harry was enthralled to see the brick walls of the three-story building with the ivy climbing to the top of the second floor. A more modern structure loomed to his left and housed the cafeteria known as the Hub. Celeste Chapeaux worked as a barista at the latte stand there.

Catching sight of her, Harry paused. She was young. Very young. Too young. She wore her hair so short it stood straight up on end and was dyed the color of a pomegranate. And she had a diamond piercing in her nose! He'd been assigned the body of a middle-aged man. Well, perhaps even a bit over middle age, wise and mature. This couldn't possibly be right. He knew that the bodies angels received were random, but still, it felt weird. He was expected to take direction from a woman barely out of her teens? This . . . this bejeweled, tattooed ruffian couldn't possibly be his lead.

She met his eyes, and it appeared that Celeste recognized Harry immediately. Her crooked smile told him she'd read his thoughts perfectly.

"Welcome, Harry," she said as she ground coffee beans. The scent of the roasted beans swirled around him. She pressed down the grounds and then twisted the small round container into the machine. She did this skillfully.

"Take a seat," she instructed, nodding toward the stool at the counter.

Still befuddled, Harry frowned and muttered, "I'd rather stand."

"Whatever."

He arched his brows. "Whatever what?"

"Whatever you want," she returned, with that same off-center smile.

The coffee machine made a horrendous noise, followed by a hissing sound that caught him unaware. Harry backed away before she set a freshly brewed Americano on the counter in front of him. He stared at the coffee, wondering what he was supposed to do with it.

"Take a sleeve; and be careful, it's hot."

"I don't need a sleeve." In fact, he wasn't sure what she was talking about. *Sleeve?*

She shrugged, again showing a decided lack of concern. "You have all the information on your assignment?"

He nodded, raised the cup to his lips, and tasted the coffee. The liquid had to be close to the boiling point and burned his lips, not to mention that the cup was uncomfortably hot to hold. Too proud to let her see, he set the cup down and then jerked his hand discreetly by his side a couple times to shake off the sting.

Celeste automatically handed him a paper sleeve, and, grumbling under his breath, Harry took it.

"You're stepping in, teaching the classic literature class."

Harry was well aware of his assignment.

"Have you read Dickens's *A Christmas Carol*?" she asked.

"Who hasn't?" he responded nonchalantly, wanting her to know he was well versed in human classic literature. Although he had reservations when it came to this particular story, especially the author's depiction of the afterlife.

"Who hasn't?" Celeste repeated. "Probably ninety-nine percent of the students in your class."

"That goes without saying. Anyway, you and I both know Dickens got it wrong. I have serious doubts about an author who so flippantly portrays heavenly spirits in such a manner. As far as I'm concerned, Dickens has taken far too much literary license. The description of Marley's ghost and the three spirits is beyond ridiculous. Someone needs to set the record straight. Humans don't actually believe—"

"Correcting misconceptions about heaven isn't part of your job," Celeste said, cutting him off.

Harry was tempted to argue, but changed his mind. He could see it would do little good. Clearly she was opinionated and most likely unable to see reason. He'd heard about angels like this, ones who were given an earthly assignment and lost their heavenly perspective. Sadly, they got caught up in the temptations of Earth. That wouldn't be a problem for him, of course.

Celeste leaned against the counter, resting her folded arms there. "Am I detecting a bit of an attitude here?" she asked.

Rather than answer, Harry posed a question of his own. "How is it you're the one in charge?"

"Do you have a problem with that?"

"Ah . . ."

"Listen, Harry, while you were strumming away on a harp I was dealing with the likes of Columbus and Lewis and Clark. Do you have any idea how difficult it was to guide *them*?"

He didn't, and stared down at his coffee. "Playing the harp isn't as easy as it looks, you know."

Celeste grinned as if to say he didn't have a clue what he was talking about. "We need to work together, got that?"

He straightened. It hadn't been his intention to start off on the wrong foot. "Got it."

"Good."

The coffee had cooled down enough for him to take a cautious second sip.

"As I said, all the necessary paperwork has been arranged. Your story is that you've accepted a transfer from Oregon State Community College. For your first assignment, you're here to help Addie Folsom. She's made a few bad decisions but is back living at home now and has enrolled in your class. Addie is dyslexic and has some serious doubts about her ability to learn. She never did well in school and fears she won't be able to do so now. Your assignment is to show her that she's smarter than she thinks and can succeed in her desire to work in the medical field. Her father was a chiropractor and she would like to follow in his footsteps. And then there's her neighbor, Erich Simmons. As a young teen, Addie had a real thing for him. That relationship might require a bit of help on your end, but don't worry. Most everything leading up to their interaction has already been set in place. Addie is going to need encouragement and a bit of direction. This first student is a test to see how well you manage before you're given the more difficult tasks."

He nodded, having already familiarized himself with the young woman's history. "I'm ready for this," he assured his earthly guide.

"Excellent. If you have any problems, come straight to me—don't attempt to handle them on your own. That's why I'm here. And let me warn you, with a human body, you're about to experience . . ."

"No need. I've got this covered. There won't be any problems . . . I've been watching Earth for quite some time. I'm ready. Really, what could be so difficult about teaching a few eager students?"

Harry might have been wrong, but it seemed Celeste's eyes widened briefly as if she struggled to hold back a laugh.

"No one ever anticipates problems," she told him, taking her index finger and drawing circles on the counter as if she needed time to recover her composure, "but they do come up on occasion. I want you to know I'm here to answer your questions and help you maneuver through this foreign landscape. What you viewed from heaven is one thing; living among humans is entirely different."

"I'm sure I'll be just fine."

"We'll see," she whispered.

That almost seemed like a challenge to Harry. Perhaps he was being overconfident. He needed to remember that she was the one with experience.

"Any other words of advice you wish to pass along?"

She seemed both surprised and pleased by his question. "As a matter of fact, there are. Don't ever forget that the world is in a fallen condition. Humans, as attractive and awesomely created as they are, tend to believe that events occur in their lives randomly, with little or no meaning. They often overlook the obvious, that God is in control."

"In other words, their spiritual understanding is limited?"

"You got that right."

"I know that."

"Fantastic." Her smile was as bright as a 100-watt lightbulb.

"Anything else?" He was eager to be on his way, find his classroom, and get started.

"A word of caution: Do what you can to never cross Dr. Conceito."

"Who?"

"The college president. He won't cut you any slack. In fact, stay away from him entirely if you can."

"Okay. Is that it?"

"Remember, human understanding is limited, and furthermore, you're about to experience . . ."

"Yes, yes, I know."

She smiled again as if keeping a secret. "And whatever you do, unless it is an absolute emergency, you must not cross the line. You say you're familiar with the parameters of your mission, now prove it."

Harry raised his hand to stop her before she said anything more. "No problem." Really, this assignment—during the Christmas holidays, to boot—was going to be a piece of rum-soaked fruitcake. A real delight. He was absolutely convinced of it.

Rushing out of the Hub, Harry eagerly started toward his classroom. The meeting with Celeste could have gone better, he thought as he took a shortcut across the lawn.

"You!"

The sharp command in the man's voice caught Harry up short. He stopped and glanced up to find a distinguished-looking man, dressed in a coat with a starched white shirt and fashionable tie, his arm outstretched, pointing directly at him.

Harry flattened his hand over his chest. "Me?"

"Yes, you. I saw you walk across the lawn."

"Ah . . . yes."

"Did you read the sign?"

"The sign?"

"The do-not-walk-on-the-grass sign."

"Oh . . . I guess I overlooked it." Extending his arm, Harry introduced himself. "Harry Mills."

The other man frowned and ignored his hand. "Harry Mills from Oregon State Community College?"

Harry nodded and lowered his arm. "Yes, one and the same."

"Don Conceito, the college president. Come to my office. It looks like I'm going to need to review the campus rules with you."

Chapter One

This wasn't the way it was supposed to happen. Six years out of high school, Addie Folsom had envisioned returning home loaded and driving a fancy car. Instead, she was limping back in a twenty-year-old Honda with close to three hundred thousand miles and her tail between her legs.

So much for the great promise of moving to Montana and walking into a get-rich-quick opportunity. She'd left Washington State with such high hopes . . . and ended up living in a leaky trailer and waiting tables in a run-down diner. It took all six of those years for Addie to admit she'd made a very big mistake. Pride, she'd learned, offered little comfort.

Oh, she'd returned home for visits at least a couple times a year. When asked pointed questions about her work in the silver mine, she'd made sure her answers were vague.

Then, last summer, her chiropractor father had died unexpectedly of a heart attack.

Addie had adored her dad as a child, but the moment she'd hit her teen years, their relationship had deteriorated. She hadn't repaired things before he'd passed away so suddenly. In retrospect, she suspected she and her father were too much alike. Both were stubborn and headstrong, unwilling to admit when they were wrong or make the effort to build bridges.

They'd argued far too often, her mother stepping in, seeking to make peace between her husband and her daughter. How sorry Addie was for the strife between them, now that her father was gone.

For now, she was home for good. Addie parked in front of the single-story house where she'd spent the first eighteen years of her life. She loved that it had a front porch, which so many of the more modern homes didn't. Normally, the Christmas lights would already be up. Her father had always seen to that the Friday after Thanksgiving. This year, however, the two arborvitae that bordered each side of the porch seemed stark and bare without the decorative lights.

Her mother must have been watching from the living-room window, because the minute Addie climbed out of the car, the front door flew open and Sharon Folsom rushed out with her arms open wide. "Addie, Addie, you're home."

Addie paused halfway up the walkway and hugged her mother close.

Sharon Folsom brought her hands up to Addie's face and smoothed back her dark brown hair. Her mother's chocolate-brown eyes, a reflection of her own, held her gaze with an intensity of longing.

Addie found she couldn't speak. It felt so good to be home, to really be home.

Her mother hugged her even tighter this time. "You said you were coming back, and I'd hoped . . ." She left the rest unsaid.

"I'm not returning to Montana this time, Mom."

"Oh Addie, really? I couldn't be happier. So you decided you are definitely back to stay?" She wrapped her arm around Addie's waist and led her up the porch steps. "It's so wonderful to have you home, especially at this time of year . . . it's the first one that's so difficult, you know."

The first Christmas without Dad.

"I talked to your uncle Roy," her mother said.

"Yes?" Addie tried hard not to show how anxious she was to hear what her mother had found out.

"He's pleased to know you're interested in health care. Your dad would have been so happy; that was what he always wanted for you. Roy said once you get your high school diploma, he'll do everything within his power to get you the schooling you need. He's even willing to hire you part-time while you're in school and to work around your class schedule."

Addie hardly knew what to say. This was an opportunity she had never expected. More than she could ever hope would happen. Now it was up to her not to blow it.

"Aren't you excited?"

Again, her throat tightened and she answered with a sharp nod. She knew that no matter what she hoped to accomplish, she'd need her high school diploma. One class credit was all she needed. Why she'd dropped out when she was so close to graduation was beyond her. How stupid and shortsighted she'd been. Her one missing credit was in literature, so she'd found a class she could take at the local community college.

B-o-r-i-n-g!

As a high school sophomore, Addie had been assigned to read *Moby-Dick*. Because of her dyslexia, she was a slow, thoughtful reader, often using her finger on the page to help her keep track of the words. Then to be handed that doorstop and work her way through it page by excruciating page had been pure torture. Following *Moby-Dick*, she'd been completely turned off to reading in general . . . although lately, after her television had stopped working, she'd gotten a couple books at the library and enjoyed them immensely. Finding pleasure in reading had given her hope that maybe . . . just maybe she could return to school.

"I already signed up for a literature class. It starts this week, which I understand is a bit unusual; apparently, it was delayed until a teacher could be replaced." Addie had thought she'd need to wait until mid-February, when the second semester began. This class was perfectly timed for her.

"You enrolled already?" How pleased her mother sounded, and her face brightened with the news.

They were inside the house now, and after removing her coat, Addie tucked her fingertips in the back pockets of her jeans. Standing in the middle of the kitchen, she looked around and breathed in the welcome she found in the familiar setting. Her mother had placed a few festive things around the house to help celebrate the season. The Advent wreath rested in the center of the kitchen table. The first purple candle had been lit.

When she was growing up, it'd been a big deal to see who got to light the candle every night at dinner, Addie or her brother. Generally, Jerry was given the honor. Oh, how her brother had loved lording it over her. He lived in Oklahoma now, was married, and worked as a physical therapist for a center that trained Olympic athletes. He'd always been athletic himself, just like his best friend, Erich Simmons, who lived next door. The two had been inseparable; any mental image of her brother also conjured up his constant sidekick and the way she'd humiliated herself over Erich.

At one time Addie had thought Erich Simmons was the cutest boy in the universe. He was a star athlete, class valedictorian, and the homecoming king. Addie hadn't thought of him in a long time and didn't know why he'd popped into her head now. As a teen, she'd idolized Erich and hadn't bothered to hide the way she felt. He, unfortunately, found her hero worship highly amusing. Oh, there'd been the usual antics when they were kids. Her brother and Erich had wanted nothing to do with her, despite all her efforts to follow them around. It wasn't until she was fourteen and fifteen that she'd viewed Erich in a different light and sent him valentines and baked him cookies. It embarrassed her no end to remember what a fool she'd made of herself over him, especially since he treated her like a jerk.

"Addie?" Her mother broke into her thoughts. "You look a million miles away."

"Sorry, Mom."

"Bring in your suitcases. I've got your old room all ready for you."

It felt wonderful to be home.

Addie unloaded her car, which, sadly, took only a few minutes. Everything she'd managed to accumulate in six years was contained in two suitcases and a couple boxes. When she finished unpacking, she headed directly for the garage.

Her mother found her there ten minutes later. "Addie, my goodness, what are you doing here?" she asked. "I've been looking all over the house for you. Are you hungry? Would you like me to fix you something to eat?"

"In a little while."

"What are you doing?"

Addie stood in the middle of the garage, surrounded by several clear plastic boxes she'd brought down from the shelves. Her father had been a whiz at organization, a trait she'd inherited. "I'm looking for the outdoor Christmas lights."

"But Addie—"

"It won't feel like Christmas without the trees by the porch lit up."

"But Addie—"

"Mom, please, let me put up the lights." Her dad would have wanted her to do this for her mother, Addie was sure. She owed him this, even if things hadn't been so good between them when he died, or maybe because of that.

"Erich offered to put them up for me, but I said no."

"Good." Perfect Erich. She bristled at the mere mention of his name. He'd always been so thoughtful and kind . . . to others. But he'd tortured her at every opportunity. For one thing, from the time they were in first grade together, he'd insisted on calling her Adeline. Addie had always hated the name. She'd never even known the great-grandmother she'd been named after. Saddling her with that name had been her father's doing, no surprise.

Her mother moved a couple steps into the garage. "Um . . . there's a reason I didn't want Erich to put up the lights."

Addie straightened. Her mother's voice revealed hesitation and a bit of apprehension. "What is it, Mom?"

"I mentioned all those firsts without your father, remember . . . ?"

"Yes." It was one of the reasons Addie had returned home when she did. She didn't want her mother spending this first Christmas without Dad by herself. Jerry couldn't get away, but Addie could. Actually, she'd been more than ready to leave Montana. Although she'd come to love the state, everything else there had proved to be less perfect than she'd hoped. Her job at the mine had fizzled out after a few months, but pride hadn't allowed her to return home so soon after her grand departure. For a while she drifted from job to job, until finally settling in at the diner. She'd made friends and the tips were good. It was easy enough to coast through the next few years.

"I didn't say anything earlier when you called to say you

were coming . . ." her mother said, interrupting her thoughts. Her mother wrung her hands.

"Mom, what is it?" Clearly there was something her mother didn't want to tell her.

"Please don't be upset with me."

This was all very strange. "Mom, please, don't worry. You're not going to upset me."

"You're sure?"

"Positive. Just tell me."

Her mother squeezed her eyes tightly shut. "I'm going on a two-week Christmas cruise with Julie Simmons."

It took a second for the information to sink in. "A cruise?"

Her mother still hadn't opened her eyes. "Julie's a widow. I'm a widow. We figured that we'd both get away this Christmas with a trip to the Caribbean. We booked a few days in Florida before the cruise as well. The sunshine and all . . . please tell me you're not upset with me."

"Of course not," Addie assured her, although her heart sank. This meant she'd be spending Christmas alone.

"Julie and I talked about it for months, and then right before Halloween we found this great deal from the cruise line and Julie said we should do it. If not now, when? I had no idea you'd be coming home, let alone for good, and . . . and, oh Addie, if you want I'll cancel the trip." Her voice became half plea and half regret.

"No way," Addie insisted, strengthening her resolve. "You're going on that cruise and you're going to enjoy every minute of it while I hold down the fort here."

"Erich offered to look after the house."

Of course he would.

"He's not married, you know, and neither is Karl."

Erich's younger brother.

As if she felt the need to keep talking, her mother continued. "Karl is dating a wonderful young woman and is spending Christmas with her family someplace back east. Neither Julie nor I have grandchildren yet, and being this has been such a difficult year . . ."

"Mom, please, you don't need to make excuses. I want you to do this. Please go."

"But you'll be alone."

"It's fine. I'll connect with a few friends and it won't be a problem. Don't worry about me."

"You're sure . . . ?"

"Absolutely positive."

"It's just that Julie and I have been so looking forward to this, and . . ."

Addie walked over and hugged her mother. "Stop. I wouldn't dream of letting you cancel this trip. It's perfect. You and Julie together on those warm sandy beaches. I'll be fine, I promise."

The relief in her mother's face was nearly palpable. Addie was sincere. She wanted her mother to get away for Christmas. "I still want to put up the outdoor lights," she said, returning to the plastic boxes her father had packed up the Christmas before and stored away.

"Oh sure, sweetheart, if that's what you want. Do you need me to help you?"

"I can do it." Among all the other valuable life lessons Montana had taught Addie, she'd learned resourcefulness. Though she'd never done it before, she'd figure out a way to string the lights on those two trees. It wouldn't feel like Christmas without them.

"I'll start dinner, then."

"Great. I'm starving."

After her mother left, Addie found the strands of outdoor lights and carted them to the front of the house. She needed a ladder, too. At five-foot-three, she wasn't nearly tall enough to reach the top.

She'd gotten everything set up when she heard the sound of a car door behind her. Standing halfway up the ladder, she glanced over her shoulder to see a bright, shiny, silver BMW parked at the curb behind her dilapidated, fender-rusting, once-blue Honda.

Erich.

Her heart sank. He was sure to make some derogatory

comment about her car, right after he called her Adeline. He might even be so obnoxious as to mention her girlhood crush on him. Even before he spoke, her teeth were clenched.

"Adeline, is that you?"

Unbelievable! "It's Addie," she said coolly.

"Oops, sorry, I forgot," he teased, when clearly he hadn't. Then he had the audacity to laugh.

She brushed a long strand of dark hair away from her face.

"Need any help with that?"

"No, thanks," she said, as she continued to wind the strand around the bushy tree. She needed no help, least of all from him. It wasn't only the teasing she'd taken as a kid that contributed to her dislike of him—that was only a small part. Erich, Karl, and her brother had often ganged up on her. Being something of a tomboy, she'd followed them, hungering to join in their fun. Instead, Erich had teased her mercilessly. It'd gotten worse as she grew older and got braces. He'd called her "live wire" and poked fun at her until she'd run and hide in her bedroom. But that was nothing compared to the way he'd stepped all over her tender, young heart.

"You home for Christmas?" he asked.

"Something like that," she answered, without looking at him.

He hesitated, and when he spoke he sounded genuine

and sincere. "Like I said when we spoke at the funeral, I'm sorry for your loss. I loved your dad."

"Yeah, me, too." The lump was back and she swallowed hard, determined not to let him see how his words had affected her. Funny thing was, she didn't remember speaking to him at the funeral. She'd been in a fog then, confused and grieving.

"Maybe I'll see you around."

"Maybe," she returned dismissively. At the moment, all she wanted was for him to leave her alone.

By the time she had the lights wound around the first tree it was pitch-dark. The only illumination came from the porch light.

A little while later, when Addie was half finished with the twin tree on the other side of the porch, her mother opened the door and called out, "Dinner's ready."

"I'm almost done," Addie promised, unwilling to quit now. She worked quietly, traipsing up and down the ladder as she moved the string of lights around the tree, stretching her arms as high as she could without losing her balance.

The Simmonses' front door opened. "Let me hand you the lights," Erich offered, crossing the yard and coming up behind her.

Addie's initial reaction was to reject his offer. She was more than capable of finishing this—she'd managed the first tree on her own. She'd rather avoid Erich's company.

"It's the least I can do to make up for calling you Adeline," he said.

"If you had to place lights on trees for every time you called me Adeline, you'd be decorating the entire Olympic National Forest."

"True enough. It's Addie from now on. I promise."

She wasn't sure she should trust him not to be a jerk, but she was tired and hungry. So while it dented her pride to accept his help, at this point, she was willing. "Okay." The second part took more of an effort. "Thank you."

His sigh was audible. "That wasn't so hard, now, was it? Come on, Addie, admit it."

"Harder than you realize."

Erich chuckled.

He continued to feed her the string of lights, and they didn't speak for several seconds. "I talked to Jerry the other day. We stay in touch on Facebook, but . . ."

Addie finished and hurried down from the ladder. "Listen, Erich. You don't need to make small talk with me. We've never really gotten along and there's no need to pretend otherwise." She guessed he felt a little sorry for her—back at home, having failed at her big adventure. In her sad, decrepit car . . .

"Fine." He held up his hands as if she'd pointed a gun at him. "You can't say I didn't try."

"Thanks for the help with the lights," Addie said, before heading into the house.

Harry watched the scene, standing beneath an evergreen tree, from across the street. Celeste stood next to him.

"What is it I'm supposed to do for these two again?" he asked, unable to hide his dismay. It had seemed like a piece of delicious rum cake earlier, but now that he saw the way Addie bristled around Erich, he was a bit more daunted. She was like a porcupine around him, defensive and unfriendly. And that was only a small part of what he sensed in her. She was full of fear, and trying desperately hard to hide her feelings of inadequacy.

"You'll find out soon enough. God has obviously crossed their paths for a reason. There must be something they need to learn from each other, don't you think?" she said, turning the question back on him.

"Just how am I supposed to help them find out what it is when they can barely tolerate the sight of each other?" he asked. He was an English teacher and Addie was in his class. There was only so much he could do while teaching her literature.

"As I explained earlier, circumstances have been set in motion."

"Yes, but—"

"Patience, Harry, patience."

"Do you have an idea about what's going to happen?"

"I do."

Harry frowned. "Don't you think you should fill me in, seeing that I'm going to be working with Addie?"

Celeste grinned. "All in good time."

Harry wasn't pleased. "Is there anything else you want to tell me?"

"Not yet," she said, and tucked her arm around his elbow, shivered, and then glanced toward the sky. "Let's get back. The roads are getting icy."

Harry watched as Erich sped off in his shiny car. He had the distinct feeling Celeste had been trying to tell him something important.

Chapter Two

The last time Addie Folsom had stepped into a classroom it had resulted in an argument with the teacher and her being escorted to the principal's office. Later that same day, she'd walked out of Tacoma High School and never went back.

In hindsight, that hadn't been a smart decision. As a result of her dropping out of school she'd had an argument to end all arguments with her father, and the shouting match that ensued could be heard three neighborhoods away. She'd been grounded: her father took the door off her bedroom, confiscated her phone, her television, her iPod, and her keys, and claimed she couldn't have any of it back until she returned to school. Addie adamantly refused. She was eighteen and headstrong. After weeks of fighting with her parents, she packed her suitcase, took back her phone and her driver's license, emptied her closet and her savings, and left home.

So it was with trepidation that she entered this classroom. Frankly, she didn't come with high expectations but was determined to give it her best shot and, God willing, pass the class and collect her high school diploma.

She hesitated only a few steps into the classroom, her heart beating fast and wild. The teacher locked eyes with her and smiled. His look seemed to be saying he'd been expecting her. Of course, it could have been Addie's imagination. The look of welcome might have been a simple gesture except that it stopped her cold. It almost seemed as if he knew her and she was the one he'd been waiting to meet.

"Addie Folsom?" he asked, approaching her expectantly, grinning broadly.

"Yes. How did you know?"

His eyes widened and he quickly glanced down, as if she'd caught him red-handed at something he knew he shouldn't be doing.

"Ah . . . you look like an Addie."

"I do?" Seeing how she felt about her name, this was depressing news.

"Oh yes. The minute I saw you, I said to myself, 'That

young woman looks like an Addie.' You're going to do very well here."

She frowned. "How do you know that?"

"I . . . just do."

He wasn't making sense, but then she didn't have great expectations when it came to classes and teachers. Experience had taught her to quickly take her seat and keep her opinions to herself, especially if she wanted a passing grade, which she did. Her one desperate hope was that he never called on her to read out loud. She had nightmares about that from grade school.

He handed her a book, which was Dickens's novel *A Christmas Carol*, and Addie found a vacant desk toward the back of the room. A man dressed in fatigues who looked to be about her age sat in the farthest desk in the row behind. A mixed-breed shepherd lay by his side, his chin resting on his paws. The dog's gaze followed her closely. The name band on the front of the soldier's shirt identified him as Fairfax. He slouched in his chair with his arms crossed over his chest and his head down. He didn't appear to be any more pleased to be in class than Addie did.

"This seat taken?"

The question caught her by surprise, and she turned to find a large, muscular man with a huge tattoo on his neck. She didn't need to be an expert to recognize it as a prison tattoo. "No, feel free," she said, and gestured toward the empty desk directly across from her.

He slipped into the seat and slumped so far down that it was a wonder he didn't slide directly onto the floor.

Other students entered the class, and before long every desk was filled. A couple high school running start for college teens took the front desks and stared up expectantly at the teacher. The teacher took a marker and wrote his name across the whiteboard:

Harry Mills.

"Any alphabet soup go with that name?" the guy with the neck tattoo called out.

The high school students twisted around and stared back at him.

"Alphabet soup?" Harry reached for a sheet from his desktop and read it, as if that would supply the answer. "You're Danny Wade, right?"

Danny's eyes narrowed suspiciously. "Has my parole officer been talking to you?" he demanded.

"No, no," the teacher assured him with a dismissive wave of his hand.

"That's crazy. How do you know who I am?"

Again, the teacher looked flustered, as if once more he'd committed some error in professional etiquette. "Lucky guess?" he suggested on a hopeful note.

"Sh—"

"No bad language in the classroom," Harry said sharply, cutting him off. "Now, what did you mean by asking me about the alphabet soup?"

"You know," Danny continued. "Like Ph.D."

"Or CPA," another student suggested.

Danny chuckled. "Looks to me like he's got a degree in BS."

The professor appeared all the more confused and simply shook his head as if he wasn't sure how to answer.

"Say, just how long have you been teaching, anyway?" someone else wanted to know.

"Well . . ." Using his index finger, Harry pushed his glasses up the bridge of his nose. "Awhile now."

A few of the students snickered. The remaining students simply stared, Addie and the vet with his dog among them. Almost immediately, someone knocked on the door. The teacher looked relieved at the interruption as a security guard entered the classroom.

He was dressed in a campus security uniform and had a Taser gun strapped on his belt. His hand rested on the handle. "Everything okay in here, Mr. Mills?"

The teacher glared at the weapon. "Yes, of course. Everything is under control."

The security guy focused his attention on the class, removed his hand from the gun, and inserted his thumbs into his waistband, rocking back on his heels. "I just like to check in on things—hope that's okay."

He glared toward the back of the room, in Addie's direction. It took her a minute to realize he was focused on Danny Wade. Addie almost felt sorry for Danny. It wasn't hard to figure out that he was on parole. It didn't look like he was going to have an easy time of it, first with the teacher and now campus security breathing down his neck.

"Officer Brady Whitall at your service," he said, and bounced his fingers against his forehead, saluting Harry. "You have any problems and you know who to call."

"Ghostbusters?" Danny muttered under his breath.

Brady's arm flew out and he pointed directly at Danny. "I heard that."

Danny looked behind him at the shepherd lying contentedly on the floor, his chin resting on his paws, and shrugged as though he didn't know what the man was talking about.

"Thank you," Harry said, and quietly ushered him out of the room.

"Now, where were we?" he asked, looking back at the class.

Thankfully, the remainder of the sixty-minute class went considerably smoother. They talked about Charles Dickens, the author of *A Christmas Carol,* and Addie had to admit she was impressed. Harry, for all his discomfort earlier, seemed familiar with the author. He clearly knew the subject matter.

"Charles was the second of eight children," Harry said, "and he fathered ten of his own. He moved around quite a bit as a child and was forced to drop out of school to help support his family when his father was thrown into debtors' prison. It devastated poor Charles."

Danny sat up straighter. "His father did time?"

Harry nodded. "Those were bleak years for his family."

"Yeah," Danny mumbled. "Were they able to write him letters? Mail is everything to a guy in prison."

"Yes, but his mother and the younger children went to prison with his father."

"You mean he had conjugal rights?"

"Well . . . yes, I guess you could say that."

"Charlie went to live with a friend of the family," Harry continued. "He did what he could to help his parents and wrote them letters of encouragement. He was smart enough to make friends with a guard, and the guard snuck the letters in to his mother and father."

"How do you know that?" one of the eager students asked. "I never read anything about Charles Dickens knowing any of the guards."

"Oh . . . I can't remember exactly where I got that information, but it happened, I can assure you of that."

Harry certainly sounded convincing, as if he knew these facts firsthand.

"Dickens had to work in a shoe-blacking factory and he hated every minute. When his grandmother died and bequeathed money to Charles's father, the family was released from prison." The teacher's face sobered and he sighed. "It gives me no pleasure to tell you what happened afterward."

"What?" Danny called out.

It was clear Danny was going to be the most vocal member of their class. He seemed to have a comment or question for whatever the teacher said.

"Even with his father employed and the family back together, Dickens's mother left him with the family friend so he could continue to work in the factory under deplorable conditions. Sadly, he was never able to forgive her for not sending for him."

"My mother bailed on us," Danny said to no one in particular. "She was on crack and the state dumped us in a foster family."

"You forgave your mother, though," Harry said, with an approving look.

Again, how he could possibly know that was beyond Addie. This was one strange man. He must be psychic—that was the only thing Addie could figure.

The class ended and Addie was surprised at how quickly

the hour had passed. She slid out of the desk and reached for her purse and book. They were assigned to read the first fifty pages before they returned to class on Wednesday.

She reached for her coat and slipped her arms inside. The vet with the dog stood and started out of the class.

"You left your coat on the back of the chair," Addie told him. He must not have heard, because he continued out of the classroom. Addie reached for the thick winter jacket and hurried after him.

"You forgot your coat," she said, louder this time, and touched his arm.

The vet whipped around, his eyes blazing fire, with a look so intense she gasped and automatically backed up, fearing he might reach out and strike her.

He blinked and immediately looked contrite. "I'm sorry . . . sorry." He grabbed his coat and hurried down the hallway, the dog trotting obediently at his side.

Addie pressed her hand against her chest in an effort to control her rapid heartbeat.

The security guard was making a fuss again, she noticed. He had a woman by the upper arm, and it seemed his hold was unnecessarily tight. The young woman looked as if she was part of the kitchen staff over at the cafeteria. She had on a white apron and wore a net over her hair. The school cop half dragged her toward the teacher.

"I found her standing outside your classroom, listening

in on the discussion," he dutifully told Harry. "It's against regulations for her to be in this building."

Harry calmly spoke to the woman in Spanish. Her dark brown eyes widened and she adamantly shook her head. She answered in a flurry of her native language. The teacher listened intently, nodded several times, and then looked at Brady Whitall.

"It's not a problem. This is Elaina; she was simply curious about a few of the classes and decided to check them out."

Brady shook his head, dismissing the explanation. "College rules clearly state that the kitchen staff must remain in their designated area."

"Yes, but I think we can make an exception this one time."

Addie wanted to cheer. Harry Mills was something of a surprise. He made the class interesting, and yes, he was a bit odd, but he was willing to stand up to this overzealous school cop.

The security guard looked doubtful. "Did you clear this with Dr. Conceito? There are regulations about this sort of thing."

"Well . . . no, but I will."

Brady inserted his thumbs in his waistband and glared at Elaina. "See that you do. Until I hear from Dr. Conceito myself, I want to make sure this doesn't happen again. Understood?" He narrowed his eyes. "You wouldn't want to lose your job over this."

The woman looked terrified. "Yes, sir, I mean, no, sir. I mean, I understand, sir."

Addie returned to the classroom to retrieve the Dickens novel, which she'd left on her desk. She watched as Harry reached for an additional copy of the book and handed it to the woman from the cafeteria. She looked so grateful that for a moment Addie thought she might actually kiss his hands. Holding the book against her breast, she spoke to him again in Spanish.

Seeing how much the other woman appreciated the book made Addie realize how fortunate she was. As she walked across campus toward the parking lot, she saw that the cafeteria remained open, although they'd finished serving for the day. Addie had eaten a light meal before heading to class and could use a latte. The wind whistled through the trees, and the moon was bright and full, casting shadows across the lawn.

Home only a few days and it felt as if she'd been back for years. It was a good feeling.

Thankfully, there wasn't a long line, so she ordered a skinny eggnog latte, which was the special for the month of December. As the barista with the name tag that identified her as Celeste made her drink, Addie slid onto the stool and removed her gloves. She reached for her phone and took it off silent, and noticed a text message from her mother.

Call me ASAP.

The last time she'd gotten a similar text from her mother it was to tell Addie her father had succumbed to a heart attack. Addie stared down at the phone, afraid of what this might mean.

The barista set the latte on the counter and looked at Addie. She must have gone pale, because Celeste asked, "Is everything all right?"

"I . . . I don't know." She didn't delay any longer but grabbed the phone and selected her mom's number from the contact list.

Her mother answered on the first ring, as if she'd been pacing the living room, awaiting Addie's call. "Addie," she said without greeting. "Is that you?"

"Yes, Mom, what's up?"

"Erich's been in a car accident."

"Erich Simmons? Is he all right? What happened?"

"I'm not exactly sure. Julie was too upset to explain it all."

"Is he going to be okay?"

"Yes, yes, apparently it could have been a lot worse. He's been injured, though. Both his wrists are broken."

Addie sighed. "That's awful." But it didn't explain why her mother appeared to have gone into panic mode.

"It's more than awful," her mother cried, sounding close to tears. "It's a catastrophe."

Addie wouldn't go so far as to say that. She sympathized with Erich, and while it would be awkward for him for a few weeks, he'd recover. This wasn't the end of the world.

"Don't you realize what this means?" her mother demanded.

Obviously, Addie didn't.

"It means," her mother said, her voice cracking, "that Julie and I have to cancel the cruise."

This wasn't making sense to Addie. "Why would you do that?"

"Why?" her mother asked, and then repeated herself. "Why? Because Julie can't leave Erich in this condition. Someone has to be there to help him. For the love of heaven, Addie, both his arms are in casts. He's going to be completely helpless."

"Oh." Addie hadn't stopped to think about that.

"Julie didn't tell me right away until she knew for certain the kind of help Erich is going to need. The accident happened the night he stopped by the house . . . when you put up the outside Christmas lights. He's out of the hospital, but he has to stay with Julie until he's able to return to work, and that will be up to six weeks. Can you imagine . . . that poor, dear boy."

Erich was no dear boy; Addie could testify to that. "I'm so sorry, Mom."

"Me, too." A soft sob escaped. "And so close to when we were set to leave, too. Julie and I have been planning this cruise for months. We both had our suitcases packed. I just knew something like this would happen. I just knew it."

Addie had rarely heard her mother sound more devastated. "That's dreadful, Mom."

"I guess it just wasn't meant to be."

Addie couldn't think of anything more to say. She was disappointed for both her mother and her mom's friend.

"There will be other cruises," Addie said, and hoped she sounded encouraging. She felt bad, but really there was nothing she could do to change this unfortunate set of circumstances.

Chapter Three

Addie dropped her phone into her purse, feeling wretched.

She noticed that her classic literature teacher had stopped by the latte stand himself. Harry Mills sat on the other side of the stand, opposite her. He sank onto the stool and braced his elbows on the counter and hung his head. He appeared to be having troubles of his own.

Celeste, the barista, ignored her latest customer and asked Addie a second time, "Is everything all right?"

Addie shrugged. Normally, she kept her problems to herself, but to her surprise she felt like talking. "The call was from my mother. She was set to take a two-week cruise over Christmas with her best friend. They're both widows and, well, there was an accident involving the other woman's son and now it looks like they're going to have to cancel the entire cruise."

"That stinks."

On the other side of the latte stand, Harry Mills straightened and looked sympathetic. "That's unfortunate."

"Is the son doing okay?" Celeste asked, looking genuinely concerned.

While Addie didn't particularly like Erich, she did feel bad for him. "He broke both his wrists."

"Wow . . . ouch."

The idea of Erich in pain had a curious effect on her. It made her stomach go queasy. She'd been looking forward to enjoying the Christmas-themed latte only minutes before, but now she felt as if she'd wasted her money.

Celeste looked toward Harry as if expecting him to say something. He stared back at her blankly as if to ask *"What?"* Addie had her money out, ready to pay for the latte, when Celeste turned back to her.

"You say your mother is disappointed?"

"That's putting it mildly." Addie's mother had sounded devastated. "My father died this summer, and the thought of spending this first Christmas without him was huge for her. The cruise was just the escape she needed."

Celeste tapped her index finger against her lips as if mulling something over. She glanced over at Professor Mills again as though waiting for him to offer a suggestion. When it appeared he had nothing to say, Addie slid off the stool, and the barista said quickly, "Perhaps there's a way for your mother and her best friend to go on that cruise after all."

Automatically, Addie shook her head. "Julie can't leave Erich. With both his wrists in casts he won't be able to do much of anything without help." It was an unfortunate situation. An idea played briefly in her mind. "I'd offer to go with Mom, but I just started classes and . . ." She couldn't afford it and she definitely didn't want her mother to pay for the cruise, and basically that was what would happen. Her mother needed her friend, a woman who'd walked that same path of grief with the loss of a husband.

"What about you?" Celeste suggested, looking her straight in the eye. "Couldn't you be the one to help Erich?"

"Me?" Addie held up her hand, stopping the other woman before she said anything more. "That would never work. Unfortunately, Erich and I have been at odds nearly our entire lives. We've never gotten along, and I don't expect we ever could."

"Why not?"

Addie shrugged. "We're different people. He drives me crazy, always has. I can barely tolerate being in the same room with him."

"He might have changed." The English teacher caught up to the conversation. "People do, you know."

"I don't think so," she said, remembering the conflicts of their youth. At one time she'd badly wanted to be friends with Erich and her brother, but they'd been set on excluding her. Then, because she felt she had to explain, she added, "Erich and I have a history that dates back to grade school, and none of it's pleasant." She remembered how, even as a kid, Erich had taken delight in teasing her mercilessly, and going out of his way to embarrass her in front of their classmates. Just thinking about how he'd treated her caused her to bristle. As much as Addie would like to help her mom out by looking after Erich so they could take the cruise, it'd never work. The mere idea was impossible.

"Didn't I hear you say you'd recently moved back into the area?" Harry asked.

Addie couldn't remember mentioning anything of the sort, but perhaps she had. "Yes."

"How long has it been since you've had anything to do with your neighbor's son?"

"A while," she admitted with some reluctance. "Six years, actually."

Harry smiled. "That's what I thought. Six years is a long time. You're not the same person you were when you left, are you?"

"No." Addie could already see the direction this conversation was taking, and she didn't like it.

"Erich isn't a teenager any longer, either."

"He hasn't changed," she argued. He might have been fairly decent helping her place the outside Christmas lights, but he was like that. Just when she felt she could trust him, he'd turn on her. One time, when she was about nine, Erich told her she could come into the fort Jerry and he had built if she ate a worm. As disgusting as that was, she would have done anything to get into that fort with them. She'd run inside the house for the can of whipped cream she knew was in the fridge. She almost gagged, but managed to let the worm glide down her throat along with the cream. And then he'd laughed and refused to let her in the fort.

It didn't get better when she entered junior high, either. Erich convinced her that one of the cutest boys in the class had a crush on her. The boy played along, making fun of her behind her back. Later, she'd learned Erich had asked for help because he wanted to distract her from following him around like a sad little puppy. All too soon the entire school was in on the joke and she'd been mortified. Oh no, Erich wasn't to be trusted.

"I guess it depends on how much you want to help your mother," Celeste added, on a sad note.

"Not really," Addie said, as she took her latte and headed off across campus. However, Celeste's last words followed her all the way to the parking lot, echoing in her head.

Caught up in her thoughts, she didn't hear anyone walking behind her until the dog barked. Glancing over her shoulder, Addie saw that it was Andrew Fairfax from class. The dog trotted along at his side.

The Army veteran caught up with her and then slowed his gait to match hers. He wore a knitted cap over his head. When he spoke he kept his gaze downward and didn't look in her direction.

"Hi," she said.

"Hi," he returned, then hesitated. "I wanted to apologize about . . . you know."

"Hey, no problem," she said, quickening her steps. He didn't seem to know what else to say. An awkward silence stretched between them, but still he continued walking with her.

"I know I scared you. I don't like people touching me . . ."

"Like I said, it wasn't a big deal."

Andrew expelled a harsh breath.

Hoping to ease the tension, Addie looked down at the shepherd and asked, "What's the dog's name?"

"Tommy."

It wasn't a common name for a dog, but Addie didn't feel she should comment. "Hello, Tommy." They paused in front of a big parking lot. Addie bent down to pet his ears. She liked animals, especially dogs.

"Please don't," Andrew said, stopping her. "He's a service dog, and it's best that you don't touch him . . . either."

"Sorry, I didn't know. What is his job?"

"The Army gave him to me . . . as a companion, to help keep me calm. I wasn't interested at first, but I've changed my mind since he's come to live with me. My sister calls him my comfort dog, and you know what? She's right. He helps."

"Good!" Addie realized she wasn't the only one in this class who came with a load of emotional baggage; knowing that helped. She had more in common with this Army veteran than he realized.

Andrew quickly headed off in the opposite direction, almost as if he couldn't get away from her fast enough. Addie suspected it had taken a great deal of courage for him to find her and apologize. The military taught you to be tough, not to be vulnerable, and yet they were both opening themselves up by taking this class, taking a leap of faith.

When Addie arrived home, she found her mother sitting in front of the television, staring blankly at the screen. A wad of crumpled tissues rested on the side table.

"Hi, Mom," Addie said, and sat down on the ottoman and reached for her mother's hands, holding them in her own.

Her mother responded with a weak smile. "How was your class?"

"Not bad."

"What do you think of your teacher?"

Addie shrugged. "He's okay, a little awkward. He seemed to know me from somewhere, but I swear I've never met the man in my life."

Her mother's knitting rested in her lap. It didn't look as if she'd had much enthusiasm for the project.

"I'm really sorry about the cruise," Addie felt obliged to say again.

A tear leaked from her mother's eyes. "Yes, me, too . . . Julie and I aren't even sure we can get a refund. We didn't pay for travel insurance . . . we were both so sure nothing would ever stop us from taking this trip."

"Oh Mom." Addie leaned forward and hugged her mother.

"The worst part is, we'll never be able to afford to do this again . . . especially without a refund."

Addie closed her eyes. She couldn't believe she would even consider making this offer, but . . . straightening, she expelled her breath and whispered, "Maybe there's something I could do to help."

"What was that look about?" Harry asked Celeste. He'd come to the Hub to reassure her all had gone well with the class and ask a few questions. When he'd arrived he'd found

Celeste chatting with Addie Folsom. Before he fully understood their conversation, Celeste had sent him a look sharper than any dagger he'd ever seen. Clearly he'd missed something important having to do with his young charge. Frankly, he hadn't had a lot of time to think about Addie. He was upset about the way the security guard had talked with Elaina. Angels weren't supposed to get upset; problems bounced off them like tennis balls in a court. This feeling was foreign to him, and he needed to ask Celeste what was happening to him.

"Harry, you should have been the one to suggest Addie help her mother."

"Me?" He felt his eyes go wide.

"Addie is your first earthly assignment. You said helping her would be easy, remember? Apparently, it's *too* easy, because you have yet to become involved."

"I'm involved," he argued, taken aback by her reprimand. It wasn't like he didn't know what to do. "I suggested that if she'd changed in the last six years, then perhaps Erich had, too," he reminded his mentor.

"Yes, and that was good."

"Thank you."

"It wasn't enough."

Harry was beginning to think he'd already messed up his first earthly mission. He needed advice. Coming to Celeste had meant swallowing his pride and admitting he might actually have overestimated his abilities. This was something else he wanted to discuss. He needed to know where this pride thing originated. He'd been dealing with it from the moment he'd landed on Earth.

Leaning forward, he braced his hand against his forehead. "Unfortunately, I've gotten myself into a bit of a situation."

Celeste braced her hands against her hips. "Okay, tell me what's happened."

"First off . . . I flubbed up a couple of times with the students. No worries there—I was able to muddle through without a problem." Then, feeling he should explain a bit more, he added, "I called the students by their names before they had a chance to introduce themselves is all. No big deal, right?" He studied her and had the distinct feeling she already knew all this.

Celeste frowned. "There's more going on here than you're telling me, isn't there, Harry?"

He nodded, unsure exactly where to start.

"It involves Dr. Conceito, doesn't it?"

"Ah . . ."

"Harry, I warned you to stay away from the school president as much as possible, remember?"

"I remember."

"And what was one of the first things you did?"

Harry didn't need the reminder. That same feeling he'd

experienced earlier—that she already knew—returned, and he cocked his head, unsure what it was.

"Harry?"

"I walked across the lawn." He pressed his hand against his stomach in order to deal with the uneasy feeling that stole over him.

"What's the matter?"

Harry blinked several times. "I'm not sure."

She gave him a knowing smile. "You can tell me."

Lowering his voice, Harry said, "I was upset earlier. Angels don't get upset. Have I done wrong . . . is that why?"

"No," she reassured him. "You've forgotten something very important, Harry. You have a human body now, not a spiritual one; therefore, you will experience human emotions. They'll be foreign and uncomfortable in the beginning, but gradually you'll learn to recognize and deal with them."

"You mean like frustration, anger . . . that sort of thing?"

"Exactly. I tried to warn you earlier," she reminded him, "but you were convinced you knew it all. Now you see."

Harry couldn't very well comment. He'd brought this on himself, walked into this without realizing what it meant to be transformed from one body to another.

Celeste gently patted his hand.

Taking a sip of his latte, Harry lubricated his throat,

which had gone dry and tight. "I met Elaina Gomez, who works in the cafeteria."

"I know Elaina," Celeste said, with a note of expectation. "She's a wonderful single mother with two little girls."

"She got caught standing outside the classroom listening in on the lecture. I sort of stepped in when the security guard was about to physically remove her from the building." Brady Whitall had been none too gentle, either. Harry suspected the guard had been waiting for an opportunity all night to get physical with someone. He was a man who seemed to be spoiling for a fight.

"That could only be Brady," Celeste said, frowning. "He's a piece of work. He tried out for the Tacoma Police Department six times and failed each time."

"I defended her and . . ." He paused as his mentor slowly started to shake her head.

"Harry, you can't do that. Your powers are limited to the students inside the class. Elaina isn't under your protection. Unfortunately, you can't help her."

"But . . ."

"No buts."

Harry wanted to argue, but he knew Celeste was right. He should never have gotten involved, especially on his first day of teaching. His downfall was he'd been touched by the gentle woman's desire to learn. She couldn't afford to take the classes, and apparently this wasn't the first time she'd been caught standing in the hallway, listening, in order to glean what knowledge she could. From their short conversation, Harry learned that Elaina was a voracious reader who liked to practice her English by reading novels. She had grabbed hold of the Dickens novel he'd given her as if he'd gifted her with a diamond.

"You realize Dr. Conceito will find out about this, don't you?"

Harry measured his response carefully. "I was thinking that maybe you could make that not happen?" His eyes were wide and hopeful.

"Sorry, Harry, I can't do that." To her credit, she did sound regretful.

Harry's throat tightened, but, wanting to downplay what had happened, he waved his hand. "I don't think there will be a problem. I can handle the school president."

"Might I remind you that unless it's a matter directly related to Addie Folsom or another one of your students, you're unable to use any spiritual powers to counteract Dr. Conceito? Didn't I warn you earlier that the man is a force to be reckoned with?" she reminded him.

Swallowing tightly, Harry nodded. "I'll do what I can to make matters right."

"Good. Don't hesitate to come to me with problems. I'll do what I can to help, but I, too, have limitations. And remember, your time here is probationary. I realize coming to

Earth has been something you've been waiting a long time for, but you need to prove yourself if you're going to stay longer than the time it takes to teach this one class."

"Got it." This assignment wasn't nearly as easy as he'd assumed it would be. He'd viewed Earth from heaven and been intrigued. Now that he was here on the other side, he found it to be quite complicated.

"By the way," Celeste asked, lowering her voice, "what did you think of Andrew Fairfax's dog?"

Harry remembered how the shepherd had remained on the floor at the young veteran's side during the class. "He's well behaved," Harry said.

Then he noticed Celeste's quirky smile and recalled how the animal's gaze had briefly connected with his own. Harry was quick to make the connection. "He's one of us, isn't he?"

Celeste nodded. "Not all angels come in human form, you know."

"Andrew needs two angels?"

"Some humans require even more."

Harry had had no idea.

"Things will get better," she promised. "I feel bad that this first class caused you problems. Focus, Harry. Remember your assignment. You should have been the one to suggest Addie volunteer to help Erich, not me." She slapped his back in a comforting gesture. "Now, there's something more you need to tell me, isn't there?"

Harry's eyes widened. "You know about . . ."

"Oh yes, Harry, I do know. Now, let's talk."

He swallowed tightly and held in a sigh. He had the distinct feeling this next issue wouldn't be so easily resolved.

Chapter Four

Harry's stomach was in knots. This was a matter no one discussed in heaven. He understood that Earth had its limitations, and that he'd have emotions, but no one had mentioned . . . this. His gut felt like an alien creature had taken up residence. He planted his hand over his abdomen, hoping that would help. Nothing could have prepared him for . . .

"Harry?" Celeste said gingerly. "You've gone pale."

"Well . . . after class I had a visitor."

"Yes, I know. Tell me about it." Celeste's look was friendly, inviting him to speak openly.

"Do you know Michelle Heath? I had no idea humans could be so . . ."

"Attractive," Celeste supplied.

"Yes, and friendly, very friendly."

Celeste's face broke into a huge smile. "Ah, yes. Well, I'm sure it's not every day she meets an unattached rather handsome man around her own age."

Harry straightened his shoulders. He hadn't thought of himself as handsome. The truth was, he hadn't given much thought to his looks; he'd been handed this body to use as a vehicle, nothing more. It had never occurred to him that how he looked mattered.

Celeste was about to say more when a student approached the coffee stand and ordered a peppermint skinny latte.

Skinny? Harry didn't have a clue what that meant, but apparently Celeste did, because she didn't hesitate. For the next few minutes the barista was busy brewing coffee and steaming milk.

While Celeste was preoccupied with the customer, Harry mentally reviewed the meeting with the French teacher. He'd been a bit shaken following the exchange between the young Hispanic woman and the security guard, which might be why his guard had been down. The classroom was empty and he had been sitting there, reflecting on what had happened and how he might have handled the situation differently.

Harry had been at his desk wondering what the ramifications would be if Dr. Conceito learned of his intervention in the incident between Elaina and the security guard. Because he was preoccupied and distracted, he didn't notice that someone was in the room—that was the only excuse he could think of that made sense. He had plenty to worry about, given the way Celeste had warned him to avoid the college president.

When Harry happened to glance up he found this lovely woman poised in the doorway. Her eyes were blue like Venetian glass, and her skin was creamy and soft like cotton. For the longest moment he hadn't been able to breathe or take his eyes off her. When she spoke, it was in this breathy sort of way that caused his skin to tingle. Right then he heard the tinkling of bells announcing danger; trouble was on the horizon.

All humans were said to struggle against weaknesses. It was all part of living in a fallen world, and Harry, while an angel, was in a human body and prone to all things human . . . like desire. This was definitely an uncomfortable sensation, unfamiliar and awkward. He'd swallowed tightly and realized he couldn't make his tongue work. His mouth didn't seem to want to cooperate, either.

Thankfully, she spoke first. "Welcome," she said, in a voice that made shivers run down his spine.

Unable to take his eyes off her, Harry managed to come to his feet and stretch out his arm in order to shake her hand and introduce himself. It demanded a monumental effort to remember his name. "Harry Mills."

She clasped his hand in her own. Hers was warm and soft. "Michelle Heath." She held on to his hand for a long moment, as if she was unwilling to let it go. "I teach the French class just down the hall," she told him.

He was so enraptured by her he forgot himself and responded in French. Being well versed in languages was a requirement for placement on Earth. Instantly, she brightened, her eyes nearly melting with appreciation.

The room felt warmer than it had been only moments earlier, substantially warmer. French was a beautiful language, and it flowed back from her lips like melted butter being gently poured over a culinary delight.

Caught in the magic of her spell, Harry found that he was incapable of responding further in either language. All he could manage was a weak grin.

Michelle sighed, as though he'd managed to completely charm her. "Your French is excellent."

"Ah . . . really? Thanks." He stuttered out a response. The tinkling bells he'd heard earlier had taken on the sound of an urgent fire alarm that insisted he evacuate the building as quickly as possible. To that effect, he reached for his briefcase and stuffed papers inside. He didn't have a clue what the papers were.

"Oh, are you getting ready to leave?" she asked.

He nodded. That was when he caught a whiff of her perfume. Closing his eyes, he breathed in the scent of roses and mist and something else so potent it sent his senses reeling.

"I won't keep you," she was saying.

Harry forced his eyes open.

"I just thought I'd stop by and introduce myself," she continued, stepping closer to Harry's desk.

My goodness, she smelled heavenly. *Heaven,* he repeated. *Think of heaven.* It didn't help. Heaven seemed a very long way away. Unable to stop himself, Harry leaned toward her and sniffed her neck.

Clearly, he'd surprised her, because Michelle released a soft gasp.

Instantly chagrined, Harry tried to explain. "I don't know what perfume you're wearing, but it's very nice."

She gifted him with one of her smiles. "It's called Divine."

"That explains it," he muttered, and reached for his coat.

Michelle sat on the corner of his desk, letting one leg dangle over the edge. "Harry . . . before you go."

"Yes."

Her eyes went wide and round. "Is there a Mrs. Mills?"

Harry paused, his hand clenching his briefcase handle in a death grip.

"Are you asking if I'm married?"

"Yes."

Harry didn't answer right away because he noticed that her eyelashes were especially long. When she blinked they seemed to brush against her cheekbones. "No . . . I'm unmarried." A wife, it was decided, would overly complicate his earthly visit. Other angels sometimes came as a couple, man and wife. Harry had been assigned to go solo.

"Surely you've been married?" she quizzed, blinking with the question, fluttering those exceptionally long lashes. It was akin to watching a butterfly take flight, and for a couple of uncomfortable seconds Harry was completely mesmerized and dumbstruck.

"Never." He was anxious to leave and get to Celeste. He needed to discuss the incident involving the security guard. And then . . . then there was this French teacher.

"You've really never been married?" Michelle followed him out of the classroom, sticking close to his side as their footsteps echoed in the hallway toward the exit. "I find that hard to believe."

Harry hadn't expected his words to be challenged. He'd assumed no one would question him about such matters. "I assure you it's the truth."

Her returning laugh was light and breezy, as if she'd been teasing him all along. "Oh Harry, I believe you. It's just that I find it hard to imagine that some lucky woman hasn't snatched you up long before now."

That was when it hit him, bull's-eye, square in the middle of his forehead. *This woman was flirting with him.* He'd heard of this when he was up in heaven.

The attraction he felt for her had been instantaneous. And now he realized it was mutual. The fire alarm became a tornado warning. Right away Harry remembered the first and most important rule. Angels don't get romantically involved with humans. That was strictly taboo.

Once he was outside, the cool evening air hit his face and seemed to free him from the spell he'd fallen under. What Harry hadn't expected when he'd arrived on Earth was that he'd be tempted. He shook himself in order to clear his head. It didn't matter how he felt about this highly attractive woman. Michelle Heath was dangerous to his mission. He couldn't allow her magnetism to distract him from what was most important.

"You heard about the Christmas concert, didn't you?" she asked, in that same soft voice that fell so sweetly from her lush lips.

"Concert?" Harry's mouth had gone dry. He'd read the notice but hadn't given it much thought.

"The college choral group is putting on a holiday performance. It's the highlight of the year. They have been practicing for weeks."

Harry hesitated, afraid of where this was leading. "I . . . I don't know."

"All teachers are required to attend," she reminded him. "Dr. Conceito is adamant about that."

Harry could feel a noose tightening around his neck. She was going to ask him to accompany her.

"We could meet in Massey Hall," she suggested ever so innocently.

Harry cleared his throat. "I'll have to check my schedule," he murmured.

"Oh please do." The entreaty in her voice couldn't be ignored.

Harry blinked, and could feel himself weakening. "Massey Hall?"

"The performance center, Thursday afternoon at four-thirty."

"Of course." His mind frantically searched for a way of extricating himself, and when he spoke, the words shot from his mouth in such a rush it was amazing anyone could understand him. "I'm teaching a class right before the concert. I doubt I could make it to the performance center on time. In fact, I'm sure I'm going to be late. I'd hate the thought of you missing part of the performance because of me."

"No worries," she assured him. "I'll save a seat for you, right next to me."

This was exactly what Harry didn't want to hear. "That'd be . . . wonderful," he said. They parted, and Harry rushed to seek Celeste's advice.

"Okay, where were we?" Celeste asked, joining him once again. "Oh yes, you were getting ready to tell me about your meeting with Michelle Heath."

"Before I do, tell me what you know about her," he said.

Celeste studied him closely. "She's been divorced for a long time, with two grown children. Be careful, Harry. Michelle's lonely and on the prowl."

Harry nodded hard enough to dislocate his neck. "I thought as much. She stopped by my classroom to introduce herself."

"You're attracted to her." Celeste's tone implied he might as well transfer straight back to the pearly gates after less than a week on Earth.

"It's more a case of her coming on to me," he assured his mentor. "She asked me to accompany her to the Christmas concert . . . I made an excuse, said I'd be late, but she insisted on saving a place for me. What do I do?" he pleaded, feeling almost desperate. His heart was pounding and his breathing had gone shallow. It was absolutely necessary that he find an excuse to get out of this concert.

"Well, Harry," Celeste said, slowly shaking her head. "It seems to me you've got yourself into a pickle."

That was the last thing he wanted to hear.

Chapter Five

Although she had twenty-four hours to think it over, Addie knew this situation with Erich was going to be a difficult one. They needed to talk, and frankly, Addie wasn't looking forward to the conversation. Her steps dragged, her feet heavy, as she crossed the matted winter lawn from her family home to the house in which Erich had been raised.

Julie Simmons opened the wreath-adorned front door even before Addie had the opportunity to ring the doorbell. Her eyes, the same shade of blue as her son's, expressed deep relief and gratitude.

"Erich's awake," she whispered. "He's home from the

hospital, but he didn't have a good night. Because it's difficult for him to get up and down, he'll need to sleep in a chair for the next couple of days . . . maybe longer."

In other words, Erich wasn't in the best of moods. For that matter, neither was Addie. She hadn't slept well, either, tossing and turning in a futile pursuit of sleep. She glanced at him and saw that both his hands from midway up his fingers to his elbows were in casts, making any kind of movement difficult. Basically, he was helpless.

The instant she'd made the offer to take care of Erich, her mother and Julie had been filled with grateful relief. They'd gushed with appreciation, thanking her over and over again.

Addie had assumed she'd feel good about being able to do this for her mother. Quite the contrary. Already she was filled with dread, and her mother and neighbor hadn't even left for the airport. If Addie hadn't been able to get along with Erich for the first eighteen years of her life, it seemed crazy to think she would now. Being his caregiver would surely prove to be her worst nightmare.

And his, too.

"Come in, come in," Julie insisted, reaching out and grabbing Addie by the elbow and practically dragging her inside the house. The door slammed in her wake.

Her reluctance couldn't have been any more evident.

Automatically, her gaze flew to Erich, who sat in the living room in a recliner, his feet raised. A hand-knit afghan covered his legs. Both wrists in their casts rested in his lap. He looked miserable and in pain. One side of his face was bruised, and his lips were swollen.

"I'll leave you two to chat," Julie said, and quickly left the room.

Addie moved into the living room and stood with her fingers tucked into the back pockets of her jeans.

"You can sit down if you want," Erich said. One eye had swollen completely shut, she noticed.

"Thanks, but no thanks." Addie preferred to stand. "If you don't mind, I'd rather stand."

"Have it your way."

"Your mother must have mentioned my offer."

"Yeah, she told me. Am I supposed to be happy about that?"

His mother was right—Erich was in a rare mood. She swallowed back a retort, doing her best to remember he was in pain and not to take it personally. She bit her tongue and managed to restrain herself from snapping back.

"I'd rather it be anyone but you," he said.

Oh, he liked adding salt to a wound.

"Trust me, the feeling is mutual."

He muttered, "I figured as much."

"Isn't there anyone else who could step in?" she asked.

At first she was embarrassed to have been so blunt. Then she figured, what was the point of hiding her eagerness to escape this situation?

"Like who?"

"Don't you have someone who cares?" Because, clearly, she didn't, and she wanted to be sure he knew it.

He rotated his head and looked away from her. "Not currently."

So much for that. "What about a friend?" She was beginning to sound desperate.

"Listen, Addie, you're not obligated to do this."

She was well aware of that.

Julie, who must have been listening in on their conversation, stepped around the corner from the kitchen. "The insurance company is providing a nurse to stop by once a day. She'll see to bathing him and so on. I asked about increasing the time she spent with Erich, you know, like a private nurse," she added, "but the cost was astronomical, far and away more than we could afford."

"My friends work during the day," Erich explained. "Even if they didn't, I wouldn't ask them to be my caregivers. Not this time of year . . . or any other time," he qualified.

All the solutions they'd tried were the ones Addie had hoped to suggest. She felt her heart sinking.

"Then I guess it's up to me." Her attitude was fatalistic at this point.

"Don't bother," Erich insisted, glaring at her. "I'll be just fine without you or anyone else."

"Sure you will," Addie murmured sarcastically. He couldn't do anything on his own. She'd literally have to spoon-feed him.

His mother dropped her voice as though that would prevent him from hearing. "He hasn't been feeling well this morning, and that makes him a little cranky. I think it might be one of the side effects from the pain medication. I know you two had your differences when you were teenagers, but you're adults now, right?"

"Right," Addie admitted reluctantly.

"I'm sure it'll be fine." Her look was strained, but hopeful. "He won't always be this . . . unpleasant, I'm sure."

"Actually, I think his bad mood is related to the fact that he's about to be stuck with me," Addie returned, mustering a smile.

Erich smiled, too, for the first time since she'd arrived, letting her know she was spot-on.

"I'll leave you two alone to sort all this out," Julie said, rubbing her palms together as though to generate heat in a room that had gone decidedly cool. "I'm going to finish packing my carry-on."

Addie moved across the living room to stand in front of the fireplace. His mother had tacked up two Christmas stockings that looked crocheted. She focused her gaze on them.

"My grandmother made those for us when I was just a kid," Erich explained. "Mom still puts them up every year, but as far as I'm concerned, they're going down as soon as she walks out the door. I can't stand Christmas."

"Fine, if that's the way you feel. I'm not going to force you into a Santa suit." Nor was she interested in discussing how he felt about Christmas decorations. She had more important matters on her mind. Gathering her resolve, she faced him and asked the most important question, the one that had been on her mind most of the night. "Can we do this?" she asked.

From the intensity of his returning look, she knew she didn't need to explain the question. It went without saying that they didn't like each other. But were they capable of putting aside their differences long enough to survive the next two weeks? It wouldn't be easy on either of them. It would be more difficult for Erich than for her, being that he was the injured party and the one in need of help. He must hate the thought of being in her debt.

"Do we have a choice?" he returned, with a question of his own.

"I don't think we do," Addie murmured. She'd spent a good portion of the night seeking alternative solutions, all of which they had already considered and eliminated before she could even propose them.

"I don't like this any better than you do," Erich said, as if it was important that she understand his point of view.

"I know, and I don't blame you. I wouldn't like it, either. The question is whether we can set aside our dislike of each other long enough to see this through." Two weeks would feel like an eternity, and the worst part was that it fell over Christmas.

Once more, Erich centered his gaze away from her, focusing on the opposite wall. "I can manage, if you can."

"I'll do my best."

He nodded and then released what sounded like a pent-up sigh. "That's about all either of us can expect."

Addie sat down on the ottoman across from him and leaned slightly forward. "I have classes three days a week. It's important that I go to those." She was going to need to focus on her studies if she planned to make a go of schooling.

"No problem."

"I'll make sure you get food and have plenty of straws, but as for anything else . . ."

"Don't worry about it."

The picture of Erich stuck with her was a humorous one. Addie did her best to disguise her amusement.

"This isn't funny, Addie. I'm miserable and cranky, and

I doubt I'll be a good patient. The fact is, other than when it's absolutely necessary, it might be best if you stayed away."

"Do you honestly think I'd want to spend more time with you than I need to?" Addie felt the heat fill her face. It seemed Erich thought she would go out of her way to be with him because she still had a thing for him. The man was living in a dream world.

"Don't go all Mother Teresa on me, got it?"

If he wasn't so serious, this would be downright comical. "Trust me, you don't have any worries there."

"Good," he said, and sighed as if their conversation had physically drained him. His eyes drifted closed and then flew open as if he'd caught himself in the nick of time.

"Did you hear our mothers decided to leave tonight?" she asked. Their flight was scheduled to leave early the following morning, and with the threat of snow, they'd decided to spend the night in an economy hotel next to the airport rather than risk missing the flight.

Erich's frown darkened his face. "Yeah, I know."

"We can do this, Erich," she said, hoping to sound positive and upbeat.

"We can try," Erich said, sounding none too confident.

Addie stood, eager to be on her way. "I'll stop by sometime this evening."

He nodded.

"I'll add my contact info to your phone—if you need anything before then, call me."

Again, he acknowledged the comment with a flippant nod. His phone was on the table next to the recliner. She reached for it and noticed several text messages.

"You have a text message here from someone named Ashley."

"I don't want to see anybody, especially Ashley."

"Do you want me to answer it for you?"

He looked up at her as if she'd suggested something weird. "No, delete them all."

"But—"

"Fine, don't. I'll do it myself later."

"Don't get snarky with me," she snapped. "I'm not your personal assistant. If you want those texts deleted, then fine. I was only trying to help."

"Just hand me my phone."

"Give me a minute," she mumbled, concentrating on adding her contact information to his device. When she'd finished and stored the number, she handed him his phone. It immediately fell out of his hand and onto the carpet. Addie reached down to get it and gave it to him a second time. He left it in his lap, leaned his head back, and closed his eyes.

"I'll be by again later."

He didn't comment one way or the other, which was just as well.

Later that afternoon, Erich and Addie's mothers loaded up the car. Addie was going to drop them at the airport hotel.

"I prepared Erich a meal," Julie was saying as she lifted the second of her two suitcases into the trunk of Addie's vehicle. In addition, she had a carry-on and a purse the size of an airplane seat. "But he didn't eat much. I think the pain meds have taken away his appetite."

"I'll check on him once I'm done dropping the two of you off," Addie promised.

"Unfortunately, when we're on the ship we won't be able to use our cell phones," his mother said, and sounded concerned.

"Don't worry, if I need to reach you, I'll find a way." Addie hoped that would reassure them both. "It should be fine, really. I'll take good care of Erich, I promise."

Once at the hotel, she helped them with their bags and check-in to make sure they had the proper arrangements to catch the shuttle first thing in the morning.

Julie gripped hold of Addie's shoulders and gave them a gentle squeeze. "I can't thank you enough for doing this. I don't know what we would have done without you."

As soon as she had her room key, Addie's mother hugged Addie close. "I hardly know what to say," she whispered, tears in her eyes. "You made this trip possible for us."

"Mom, you'd do it for me. Now go, and promise me you'll have the time of your lives."

"We will," Julie assured her.

"I'll buy you something wonderful from one of the islands," her mother said.

The two women chatted like monkeys as they headed off to their room. Her mother was as excited as Addie had ever seen her. You'd think they were schoolgirls from the way they giggled.

After dropping them off, Addie returned to the house and parked out front.

She stood outside for several minutes as the wind and winter cold whirled around her. She dreaded another confrontation with Erich, but it was unavoidable. From a few hints his mother had let drop, Erich was still in a bear of a mood. He hadn't exactly been Prince Charming earlier, and it sounded like his temper hadn't improved.

In other circumstances, she would simply walk away and let him suffer, but she had an obligation to see to his needs, whether he wanted her around or not. Perhaps she could reach out to Ashley. From Erich's response when he learned about the text messages, it was clear they'd had some kind of falling-out.

Addie hadn't read the full text, but it appeared Ashley was terribly, terribly sorry and wanted to make amends. Perhaps the ever-so-contrite Ashley might be willing to step into Addie's place as caregiver to the injured Erich. With that thought in mind, she headed toward his house.

The lights were off, and Addie feared he might be asleep. No matter, it was too early for bed. If Erich went to sleep this early in the evening, he'd be awake in the middle of the night and soon his entire schedule would be off balance.

After one polite knock, Addie let herself into the house. "I'm back." she said, coming into the living room.

He was still in the chair—she could make him out in the gloom. He ignored her.

"Can I get you anything?"

"No."

His mother was right. Erich was set on being difficult, if not downright impossible.

"You're sitting in the dark."

"So?"

"Would you like me to turn on the lights?"

"If I wanted the lights on, I'd do it myself."

She sighed. "You're getting snarky again."

Silence.

"If we're going to make this work, Erich, we're going to have to be civil to each other."

"Okay, whatever. As you might have guessed, I'm not in the best of moods."

"No kidding."

He ignored her comment. "The thing is, I'd rather be left alone."

"Feeling sorry for yourself isn't going to help, you know." Experience had taught her as much.

He didn't respond, so Addie reached for the lamp and turned the switch. Bright light instantly flooded the room. Erich squinted until his eyes had time to adjust to the change.

"Your mother mentioned that you hadn't eaten much. Can I get you anything?"

"No. Thanks anyway."

That was a slight improvement. "You'll feel better if you eat something."

"Thank you, Dr. Oz."

"It's the truth, especially when you're on pain meds. Most prescriptions are best taken with food."

"There you go again with the medical advice."

Ignoring him, Addie went into the kitchen and opened the refrigerator, looking for something Erich could eat without the need for utensils. She found an orange, which she peeled and laid out in sections on a paper towel.

"What's that?" he asked, when she returned.

"What does it look like?" she returned, and set it on his lap.

He ignored the question. "Addie, you still can't take a hint. What part of 'no thanks' do you not understand?"

That was a low blow, and completely unnecessary. If he wanted to be nasty, then fine, she'd let him. Addie sighed expressively, and then before he could stop her, she grabbed his phone off the side table. Walking to the other side of the room, she tapped the screen of his phone a couple times.

"Addie?" he shouted after her. "What are you doing?" This was followed by a few choice words she was sure would shock his mother.

Addie walked around the corner where Erich couldn't see her.

"Hello, is this Ashley?" she said, loud enough to be sure Erich could hear her. "I'm a friend of Erich's. He's been badly hurt. It's a matter of life and death, and he's begging to see you one last time."

Chapter Six

"Addie?" Erich's growly voice was low and angry. "What have you done?"

Addie stuck her head back around the corner and, holding the phone in her hand, smiled sweetly back at him. "What have I done? Why, Erich, I've shown you proof positive that two can play at that game. Oh, by the way, Ashley sounds terribly, terribly upset. She wanted me to reassure you she'll be here as soon as she can. Is there anything else you'd like me to tell her?"

"Give . . . me . . . the . . . phone," he demanded, speaking each word slowly and distinctly. "Give me the phone, otherwise I swear . . ." He started to get out of the recliner but was struggling to stand up without being able to use his arms. He looked like he was about to hurt himself.

"Oh, for the love of heaven," Addie said, returning to the living room. She handed Erich his phone.

He tried to grab it, but with limited use of his fingers, it fell to the carpet.

Addie retrieved it for him. "Stop freaking out. I didn't call her; there's no one on the other end of the line."

His relief was instantaneous.

"But I should have called her. It was what you deserve for being so difficult."

He continued to glare at her with a look that would have made other women run for cover. Not Addie.

"Listen," she said calmly, "this won't work if you're going to continue being so immature. It's only for two weeks. You can manage to be agreeable for that short amount of time, can't you?"

He exhaled slowly. "Me? You're just as immature as I am."

"That's a matter of opinion. I'm not the one behaving like a five-year-old."

Erich took a moment to consider her words and then shrugged. "Okay, you're right, I was acting a bit childish. Can we start over?"

Addie hadn't expected a concession on his part and did her best to hide her surprise. Sitting down in the recliner next to his, she reached for the remote control. "Do you ever watch *Jeopardy!*?"

"Some."

She flicked a look in his direction. "I suppose you get all the answers right."

"Not all."

She snickered. "Modesty doesn't become you."

He chuckled again. "I'm not that smart, although it does my ego good that you seem to think so."

She rolled her eyes. "Don't let it go to your head."

"No problem there, considering the source."

Addie decided to ignore the comment and changed channels until she found the right station. They sat in silence, except for calling out answers when they knew them. Not surprisingly, Erich got far more than she did. If they'd been keeping score, by the end of the game show his total would have been well ahead of hers.

When the show finished, Addie stood. "Can I get you anything before I leave?" She had homework yet and was determined to read the assigned pages, no matter how long it took.

His face revealed regret, as if he would have liked her to stay, although it went without saying he'd never admit it. "I'm fine, but thanks for asking."

"See, that wasn't so hard, now, was it?"

"What?"

"Being civil."

He frowned. "I can be civil if you're civil."

She held up her hand. "No problem. Now, before I leave, do you have your phone close at hand so you can call if you need anything?"

"Right here." He patted it, indicating it was well within reach.

"Okay." She got all the way to the front door and then hesitated. This probably wasn't the time or place, but curiosity took hold and got the better of her. "Can I ask you something?"

He seemed surprised by the question, and shrugged. "I guess."

"What's the story with Ashley?"

He groaned. "I should have guessed you weren't going to go quietly into the night."

Addie was curious, but not at the expense of this fragile peace. "Forget I asked," she said, and held up her palm in an effort to keep him from explaining. "It's none of my business."

"Thank you." He seemed genuinely grateful to find she was willing to drop the subject. It was plain that whoever Ashley was or had been at one time remained a sore spot with him.

Addie reached for the door handle. "I'll see you in the morning."

"Sleep tight," he called out after her.

"You, too."

"Not much chance of that. I much prefer a bed over this chair."

Addie didn't blame him. Not only was he in pain, but sleeping in a chair was bound to be uncomfortable. No wonder Julie had mentioned Erich hadn't slept well the night before. Addie wished there was something more she could do to help, only there wasn't. Erich had basically told her he didn't want her going all Mother Teresa on him. He'd hate it if she started hovering.

Once Addie was in her own home, she brewed a cup of tea and settled in the chair that had once been her father's favorite. It still carried a faint scent of him, and she found comfort in that. How she wished she'd made a stronger effort to reconcile with him. For a long time she simply sat with the Dickens novel in her hand, thinking about her father.

From childhood, Addie had been described as different. She'd struggled the first few years in school until she was tested and learned she was dyslexic. She still remembered when they gave her parents the diagnosis; Addie was in second grade, and in her mind, if she was going to be told she wasn't the same as everyone else, then she would be as different as different could be. In order to stand out and find her own identity, she'd purposely chosen to wear mismatched clothing and cut her own hair. Her mother defended her and claimed Addie liked to march to the beat of a different drum, although she was never entirely sure what that meant.

Her grandmother called her eccentric. Once she figured out how to spell it, Addie looked the word up in the dictionary. She discovered it came from a geometry term and one definition was "not having the same center."

The way she figured it, she was always a little off-kilter. Her grades improved, but school had never been her thing. While in elementary school she felt like she was being suffocated, and after a while, young as she was, she decided she could only be herself. She would never fit in with the norm. Pretty deep thoughts, she realized, for a girl barely eight.

Perhaps it was egotistical of her, but Addie liked to think of herself as uniquely shaped. Gifted, but not in the traditional way. As a result, she often clashed with authority figures, but no one more than her headstrong father.

She missed him. She missed him terribly. For years she'd

avoided talking to him. Now it came as a shock to realize the one she'd hurt, the one she'd been so intent on punishing, hadn't been her father, but herself.

Addie ran her hand down the chair arm as if giving a silent apology to the father she had never fully appreciated.

Sighing now, and feeling a bit maudlin, she looked around the house at all that was familiar. Although it was only a week away, it didn't seem like Christmas, although there were signs of it throughout the neighborhood. Several of the houses down the street had decorated with a dazzling display of lights. The single string around each of the two small arborvitae in the front of the house seemed like a meager effort. In past years, the whole house would have been decorated, top to bottom, inside and out. The Christmas tree would be up, with an array of cheerfully wrapped gifts stored at its base.

Not this year.

Her mother had escaped to a tropical paradise and Addie was alone . . . well, other than Erich, who wanted nothing to do with Christmas.

Her tea had cooled considerably before Addie tackled her reading assignment. She had fifty pages of *A Christmas Carol* to read before her next class. Even then, the text lay open in her lap as she considered her teacher and fellow classmates.

Mr. Mills was knowledgeable enough despite being a bit odd. He certainly wasn't like any teacher she'd ever known. She liked his style, though. He brought Dickens alive, giving them the details of the author's life, giving him a story of his own.

It was a tall order keeping the students engaged. Addie suspected that, like her, a number of the other students had signed up for the class because they needed the credits in order to receive their high school diplomas.

For sure, Danny, who'd served time in prison. She couldn't help wondering about his story. He was a kick, chiming in with an opinion for nearly everything discussed. It was a bit much, but still he was a likable guy.

Andrew, the Army vet with the shepherd, was another interesting character. Addie wondered what had brought him there. She doubted he was in need of a high school diploma. He seemed to be in need of something above and beyond what was taught inside a classroom.

The security guard . . . it took her a moment to remember his name. Brady something . . . was almost a caricature of a mall cop. Just thinking about him caused her to frown. He'd been so rude to the woman from the cafeteria when it wasn't necessary.

Her thoughts continued to wander from one subject to the next until Addie realized this daydreaming was all a delaying tactic to avoid reading the Dickens novel. It was sure to be wordy and boring, but then on the bright side, she already knew the story.

"What's wrong with me?" she said aloud. She'd been excited by this class. Perhaps *excited* was overstating her enthusiasm, but it had been years since she dropped out of high school and she'd been hopeful she could make it work this time.

It came to her then.

Addie was afraid.

The thought amused her. Gutsy girl Addie was afraid of failing, afraid that six years out of high school she not only would have the same problems getting through a lit class, she'd also flounder yet again, struggle with reading and comprehension.

Maybe she wouldn't have to read the entire book. Just the beginning to get the hang of the story, which she pretty much knew anyway. If necessary, she could watch the movie. There'd been several adaptations produced over the years. And surely there was a study guide available she could purchase through the bookstore. For that matter, there might well be online help. With all these resources, she should be able to muddle through. It was time to face those fears head-on and quit flirting with thoughts of failure.

With that mind-set, Addie turned the page and started

the book. It wasn't exactly easy reading, she decided, but it wasn't all that difficult, either. If Dickens was alive, she wondered how his ego would handle her opinion of his much-loved classic. Truth was, she found the author far more fascinating than his writing.

At some point, she must have fallen asleep, because she woke with a start and then realized that irritating noise was her phone.

"Hello," she muttered, and rubbed her free hand over her eyes.

"Did I wake you?"

"Who is this?" she asked, and then realized it was Erich on the other end of the line. Instantly alarmed, she sat up so straight that she nearly slid off the edge of the cushion. "Are you okay?"

He ignored the question. "You doing anything?"

The question was innocent enough, but Addie read between the lines and they said plenty. He was in trouble. "No. Now answer me. What's wrong?"

He hesitated.

"Erich, I mean it; what's wrong?" She didn't know what had happened, but clearly something had. It had probably killed him to have to call her.

"Okay, okay, if you must know. I've fallen and I can't get up."

Chapter Seven

Addie made it across the yard to the Simmons family home in record time. Thankfully, the front door remained unlocked. She made a mental note to lock it behind her next time. Right away she noticed the interior was completely dark.

Just inside the house, she paused and called his name. "Erich."

"Leave the lights off," he shouted from somewhere distant. It sounded as if it'd come from the hallway or the kitchen.

Leave the lights off? "Why would I do that?" she demanded, blindly searching the wall for a light switch. She hadn't been inside his home often enough to remember where it was situated.

"Just do what I ask." Erich sounded none too happy.

"No way. I'm not stumbling around in the dark." She found the switch by the door and flipped it on. The small entry was quickly ablaze in light.

"You had to do it, didn't you?" he grumbled.

Addie searched the living room, where Erich had been sitting when she left. The footrest on the recliner was down and the blanket he'd had over his legs was puddled on the floor.

"Where are you?" she called out, coming farther into the house.

"The hallway. Leave the hall light off," he demanded, and then, in a voice so soft she barely heard, he added, "Please."

He must have hit his head to request anything so nonsensical, but in an effort to keep the peace she did as he asked. "Any particular reason I won't need to see where I'm headed?"

"Several," he muttered. "Mainly because this is humiliating enough without you seeing me sprawled across the floor in my underwear."

"O-k-a-y." Now she understood. He appeared to be sitting on the hardwood surface at the far end of the hallway by the entrance to the bathroom. The dim light from the entry illuminated his outline.

"What happened?" she asked, stepping closer. She wondered if the pain medication had made him a bit unsteady.

"You don't want to know." His robe was open and spread out around him on the floor like a skirt around a Christmas tree.

"Of course I want to know," she said, moving to the side and leaning against the wall, being careful not to trip on him or the robe.

"Well, I don't want to tell you. Can you kindly leave it at that?"

She walked all the way around him in an effort to evaluate the situation. While unsure exactly how he'd gotten into this position, she could understand his predicament. Without the use of his hands, it would be nearly impossible for him to get to his feet unaided.

"If you could just help me raise myself enough to use my legs, I should be fine," he said, frustration evident in his voice.

Addie suspected he'd called her as a last resort once he'd exhausted his own strength and resources. "How long have you been like this?"

"Awhile." He was back to growling responses. "Can you please get me to my feet before I answer your questions?"

As Addie assessed things, she decided the best way to manipulate him to a standing position was from behind. She moved around to his back side and slipped her arms under his. "You ready?"

"I was ready an hour ago," he muttered.

Using every bit of strength she possessed, Addie strained to lift him enough to give him leverage to get to his feet. Despite her best efforts, he didn't budge.

"Good heavens, just how much do you weigh?" she asked, breathing hard.

He grumbled a reply. From what she could make of it, he wasn't discussing his weight.

"Temper, temper," she chided.

"It isn't you who's as helpless as an infant," he reminded her.

He was right. This situation must be mortifying for Erich. There'd been a time when she would have gotten a great deal of pleasure seeing him down and helpless. She didn't feel that way any longer. It was far too easy to see herself in a similar situation.

"Let's try again," she suggested. "This time I'll put a little more oomph into it."

Erich snorted sarcastically. "You mean to say the first attempt was just for practice?"

"Quit complaining. I'm doing the best I can." If the initial try was any indication, she could see getting Erich to his feet wasn't going to be easy.

She tried again, straining her muscles for all she was worth. Clenching her teeth, she tilted her head back, grunted hard, and gave it her all.

Nothing.

She couldn't lift him so much as an inch off the floor. He was a huge guy—easily six-three. He'd clearly continued to work out after high school and was as broad and muscular as ever. Given that she was slight, lifting him was sure to be a challenge.

Exhausted now, she slumped down on the hardwood surface, her legs stretched out in a wide V.

"Are you hurt?" he asked, glancing over his shoulder.

"No, but this isn't working."

"No kidding, Sherlock."

After Addie caught her breath she crawled on her hands and knees around Erich so that they could talk face-to-face. Her eyes had adjusted to the dark and she noticed he'd modestly tucked his robe around his front.

"You have any other ideas?" she asked. Maybe, with his engineering background, he might offer a couple of other suggestions.

He leaned his head back and expelled a grating breath. "Unfortunately, not a one."

Although she couldn't see his face that clearly, from the way he spoke, she could tell he was exhausted.

This was a last resort, but Addie felt she had to suggest it. It went without saying, Erich would object. "If worse comes to worst, I could always call for help."

"Who?"

That was a legitimate question. Knocking on the neighbors' doors would most likely mean rousing them from bed. Then Addie had an idea.

"Nine-one-one would be my first option. Firefighters are trained for situations just like this." The more she thought about it, the more sense it made.

"No way." Erich's response was sharp and automatic. He wasn't even willing to listen.

"Come on, Erich, you're in an impossible situation here."

"I am not going to have a bunch of firefighters see me in my underwear." Just the way he said it left no room for argument.

"Okay, okay." Addie held up both her hands as if surrendering. "A man and his pride."

He sat pouting for several seconds before he muttered, "Pride's all I've got left, and I'd rather keep it, if you don't mind."

Despite their differences through the years, Addie felt

bad for him. "Then we'll think of some other way." She tried to sound confident although it was more bluff than any real sense they could successfully pull this off.

They waited a few minutes in order for them both to catch their breath. Thirty minutes passed along with several attempts, all of which ended without success. They'd been nearly successful with a chair, but it was plain that putting too much pressure on his arms was not an option. When she saw the considerable pain on his face, Addie put a stop to it.

"You're hurting yourself."

"I don't care."

"I do," she argued, and pushed the kitchen chair aside, refusing to let him do any further damage to his broken wrists.

Addie slumped down on the floor, knees bent. She was too tired to stand up. "Any other bright ideas?" she asked.

"One." He chewed on his lower lip as though giving this some additional thought.

"Don't keep me in suspense," Addie chastised. "Tell me."

"If I can get to my knees."

"We tried that with the chair," she said, cutting him off.

He waved her objection aside. "The chair didn't work, but if you gave me your arm, I might be able to lift myself up enough to kneel."

"Not with your hands!" She was aghast he'd even make such a suggestion.

"Not with my hands," he agreed. "Just hold out your arm."

Addie wasn't sure what he meant until he showed her. He wanted her to hold her forearm out like a trapeze bar. She did, using all her strength to hold it stiff as a support for his own forearms to wrap around her one, and with that he was able to shift his weight enough to get to one knee. Then, gradually, the other. Soon he was upright.

After a long series of failed attempts, Addie wasn't sure why they hadn't thought of this earlier. It'd worked. It hadn't been easy, nor was it pretty, but it did the trick.

For the longest moment, they stood facing each other, too stunned to speak. Both their shoulders heaved with exertion.

"We did it," Addie whispered. "We actually did it."

"We did," Erich agreed, and then he started to sway.

In half a heartbeat, Addie was at his side with her arm wrapped around his waist. He felt warm and muscular, and she kept him close to her side, offering him her strength, which admittedly was pretty shaky. "Let me help you back into the recliner."

"Give me a minute," he said, and sounded pitifully weak.

"Sure."

He dragged in several deep breaths. "I never thought I'd have the opportunity to say this, but thanks, Addie. I'd never have managed getting off that floor without you."

"No problem."

He chuckled softly. "I beg to differ; it was a major problem."

Because he was exhausted, she kept her arm tucked around his waist, and walked with him back into the living room. Once there, he eased himself into the recliner. Without asking, she left him long enough to go into the kitchen and bring him a glass of water. She found a straw and brought it out with her.

"Here," she said. "This should help."

He had the blanket over his legs. "Thanks."

She set the water down on the tray where he could lean forward and sip without the necessity of using his hands. She waited long enough to make sure the water was close enough. Even then she was reluctant to leave, but she didn't have a good excuse to linger.

"Would you like anything else?" she asked, easing her way toward the front door.

"Nothing, thanks."

She rubbed her palms together. "Then I should probably get back."

He nodded. "Would you mind turning off the light on your way out?"

"Sure." She headed into the foyer and flipped the switch she'd turned on when she'd first entered the house. The area went dark. Addie's hand was on the doorknob when Erich spoke.

"I met Ashley in college."

She froze, uncertain if she should comment, ask questions, or simply pretend that she hadn't heard him. Curiosity won out, and she decided to learn what she could. "Ashley seems to have been important to you at one time though."

"At one time," he agreed.

"You broke it off?"

"No, she did. I had never been in love . . . well, not like this, and I took it hard. It didn't take me long to realize she'd been using me. Later she made an effort to patch up the relationship, but by then I knew being with her wasn't worth the heartache. Frankly, I don't care if I ever see her again."

"When was the last time you saw her?"

"About six weeks ago. She has a hard time taking no for an answer."

In other words, this was an on-again/off-again relationship that had dragged on for several years. Apparently, they were in the off-again cycle.

"Do you love her?" she asked, then realized that was far too personal a question. "I'm sorry," she added quickly. "You don't need to answer that."

"I did love her," he said, his voice dipping slightly, "at one time." It seemed talking in the dark evoked confidences. "But not anymore," he added.

"You don't sound that sure of yourself."

His responding laugh was wry. "Let me put it like this: I had to learn my lesson about Ashley more than once. I got the message loud and clear the last time."

Addie moved all the way back into the living room. "I guess we all go through that kind of rejection at some point or another."

"You, too?" he asked, keeping his voice soft and low.

"Big-time." Funny, a few months earlier she would never have admitted this, least of all to him. "I moved to Montana and met the love of my life. Some love. Some life. The relationship didn't last six months. If I'd been smart I would have packed my bags and headed home right then, but oh no, I wasn't about to put on my big-girl pants and admit I'd been wrong. I refused to give my dad the satisfaction, and so I stuck it out, freezing in the winter in a leaky trailer."

How foolish she'd been. How stubborn.

"We all make mistakes," Erich said sympathetically. "The key is learning from those mistakes and not repeating them."

Addie hadn't expected him to show this much self-awareness. "What mistake did you make with Ashley?"

He took his time answering. "It wasn't just one; it was several. I fell for a pretty face, but unfortunately she didn't have the heart to go with it. She was the sun of her own universe. It took far longer than it should have for me to recognize how shallow and vain she is."

Actually, now that she thought about it, Addie was fairly sure she had seen the beautiful Ashley one Thanksgiving when she'd flown home to be with family. As she recalled, Erich had paraded her into the house as if she were on a fashion runway. She'd been dressed all in bright, flashy colors that made her stand out wherever she might be.

In an effort to be generous, Addie suggested, "She might have changed."

"Doubtful." He dismissed that out of hand.

Addie had a small confession to make. "I didn't read the text she sent, but I did see the word *sorry*."

He sighed. "Ashley can't stand the thought of not having the last word. I was the one who got away, and she will say or do anything to get me back just so she can dump me again. I've seen her do it with other men and I refuse to play that game. Apparently, there was a report of my accident in the newspaper and she read it."

"Oh."

"You asked about her. A few hours ago you would have had to torture the information out of me."

"And now?"

"Now . . . I guess you earned the right to know. I appreciate your help tonight. I mean it. Thanking you hardly seems adequate. Telling you about Ash is my way of . . . I'm not sure . . . letting you know I trust you, I suppose."

Addie sat in the recliner next to Erich. She didn't know what to say. Twenty-four hours ago she would have said this transformation in her relationship with Erich would have been impossible. After years of ill will, it came as a shock to realize she might not actually dislike him. She might even be able to look past the fact that he'd broken her tender heart all those years ago.

"Are you going to say anything?" he asked, after an awkward silence.

"Wow."

"Wow?" he repeated.

She waved her hands. "In case you hadn't noticed, something has happened between us."

"Excuse me?"

"We're talking."

"Yeah, and your point is?"

"We're talking, like two normal people. We aren't arguing or sniping at each other. I . . . might even discover that it's possible to get along with you."

He laughed as if that was one of the funniest things he'd

ever heard. "Don't let this go to your head. You make it sound as if the next thing you know we'll be kissing."

"That ain't gonna happen," she assured him.

His amusement faded. "Frankly, I don't know that I'm willing to rule it out."

Chapter Eight

Thursday evening was the dreaded Christmas concert. Harry had been uneasy about it from the moment Michelle Heath, the French teacher, had mentioned she would save him a seat next to her. But now he had other, bigger worries.

In fact, the concert and his fellow instructor were the least of his troubles. Dr. Conceito, the college president, had asked to meet with Harry. They needed to have a little chat, or so he'd been told.

By comparison, the concert was sure to be like a stroll in a winter wonderland. Harry enjoyed music, although Earth couldn't compare to the thunderous choir of angels who sang praises in heaven. Now, that was some kind of performance. The music was simply "out of this world" and completely unlike anything heard on Earth.

For the last twenty-four hours Harry had managed to avoid talking to Michelle. They'd passed each other in the hallway now and again, but either he or she had been caught up in a gaggle of students each time.

As Harry passed, she raised her hand and called out, "See you later."

A sense of dread settled over Harry. If his attendance wasn't mandatory, he would have skipped the performance and made excuses later. However, Dr. Conceito had made it abundantly clear that Harry's presence was more than expected; it was demanded.

Dr. Conceito.

Although he'd been on the job only a few days, Harry had come to appreciate Celeste's warning regarding the college president. The man was more than a stickler for the rules, he was a tyrant. Even while on his best behavior, Harry had already had two run-ins with the school's dictator.

It seemed Dr. Conceito walked the halls looking for infractions with the same enthusiasm with which an anteater seeks out insects. He had a nose for it and a cohort in the security guard who took delight in reporting any behavior that appeared the least bit suspicious.

No doubt Dr. Conceito had heard from Brady Whitall, the security guard, about the cafeteria worker Harry had championed. Really, what harm did it do if the dear woman stood in the hallway and listened in on a literature class?

Angels weren't accustomed to being nervous. Heaven was serene and calm. No worries, be happy. He'd made the assumption that it would be similar on Earth. Not the same, of course, but he'd expected that being in the very center of God's will equated smooth sailing. He'd been wrong. And then there was the whole issue of dealing with human emotions . . . like attraction. Harry had yet to figure out how he was going to avoid sitting next to the French teacher at the concert.

With his heart pumping hard against his ribs, Harry entered the administration building and headed toward the president's office, hoping to get this meeting over as quickly as possible. Dr. Conceito's assistant looked up when he entered the room.

"Harry Mills," he said, as a means of introducing himself. "I believe Dr. Conceito is expecting me."

The assistant, a middle-aged woman whose thick, dark hair was streaked with gray, continued to stare at her computer screen. The name plate at her desk identified her as Patricia Ziglar. "Ah yes, here you are. If you'd kindly take a seat, Mr. Mills. Dr. Conceito shouldn't be long."

"Thank you." Harry claimed a chair and, hoping to look casual and relaxed, crossed his legs. In his nervousness, his calf slipped against the fabric of his pants and his foot thumped against the floor.

The assistant's eyes caught his, and Harry grinned nervously.

"Not to worry," the woman assured him kindly. "Dr. Conceito's bark is worse than his bite."

The college president was going to bark at him? Knowing this did nothing to settle his nerves. Earlier in the day, Harry had tried to find Celeste but couldn't. The limitations of Earth could be downright frustrating. In heaven there was no such thing as distance or, for that matter, time. Everything flowed together. Nothing was ever lost, nor did he need to look for someone. All he had to do was think and they were there. So easy. So convenient.

Earth was at a grave disadvantage, and sadly, humans had yet to realize it.

A buzzer went off on Patricia's desk. She looked back at Harry. "Dr. Conceito will see you now."

Harry leaped to his feet as if the chair came equipped with a huge spring that propelled him upward.

"It'll be fine," Patricia whispered, as she escorted him to the door with the frosted-glass window.

Harry stepped inside and the assistant closed the door

behind him. He glanced over his shoulder at the clicking sound, then turned his attention to the college president. "You asked to see me?"

"Yes," Dr. Conceito said, and motioned toward the chair in front of his desk. "Take a seat."

Obediently, Harry sat. Perhaps it was better that Celeste not know about this meeting. He'd already gotten on the negative side of the man by walking on the grass, getting caught red-handed. The president's reaction had made it seem that Harry had taken a machete to bushes and desecrated the landscape of the entire campus.

Dr. Conceito leaned forward in his high-backed desk chair, pinning Harry with his gaze. "I got a report about you from Officer Brady Whitall."

Officer?

"I have to assume this is in regards to Elaina Gomez?" Harry asked, presuming innocence.

"Yes," the college president confirmed. "In case you weren't aware, it's strictly against school policy for an employee to leave their position while the kitchen is still open."

"I understand," Harry said. Elaina had explained that she'd managed to finish cleaning up early and her supervisor had dismissed her for the night. Because she had extra time before the bus arrived, she'd come to listen to the lecture in Harry's class. "But—"

"There are no *buts* at this school," Dr. Conceito said,

interrupting Harry. "The rules are the rules, and bending them even the slightest amount is unacceptable."

"I understand, however—"

"Furthermore, I am told this woman was listening in on your lecture."

If the school president was looking for evidence to take away Elaina's job, Harry was determined not to give it to him. "That I wouldn't know."

"Did you or did you not see her outside the classroom?" he pressed.

"I did, but only after the class was dismissed."

"Not before?"

"No." Harry could say that in all honesty.

Dr. Conceito thumped his fingers against the desktop as if weighing his options. He sighed and then said, "I was also informed that you gave Ms. Gomez a copy of the Dickens novel *A Christmas Carol,* which I understand the class is currently reading."

"Yes—"

"You do realize the book is school property." This was more statement than question.

"Yes, but—"

"Mr. Mills," Dr. Conceito said, impatiently interrupting him a second time. "What did I just tell you about *buts*?"

Harry looked down in an effort to avoid eye contact. "There are no buts at this school."

"Correct. Now, would you like to rephrase what you were about to say?"

Harry took a couple moments to collect his thoughts. "I wanted you to know that I stopped off at the bookstore to personally pay for the copy I gave Ms. Gomez."

"That's unnecessary," Dr. Conceito insisted, his face tightening.

Harry was undeterred. "It's my feeling we should encourage reading at all ages and economic levels."

"I agree," the school president said. "Tell me, did the bookstore accept payment?"

"No."

The grin on Dr. Conceito's face revealed no real amusement. "Did they give you a reason they wouldn't take your money?"

Harry didn't know where this conversation was going. "No, they didn't."

The smile disappeared. "Then let me keep you abreast of the results of your actions."

Harry leaned back and tried to appear to be relaxed. "Yes, please do."

Dr. Conceito exhaled sharply. "First off, you should know that I was required to visit Ms. Gomez and ask for the return of the novel."

Harry's shoulders sank, picturing the disappointment

the young mother must have felt, having to return the book she'd accepted with such appreciation and excitement.

"I was willing to pay for the book," Harry reminded the president.

"That is unacceptable," Dr. Conceito argued. He stood and leaned toward Harry, planting both hands on the desk. "In case you are unaware, the Dickens novel was part of a government grant. To freely hand it out indiscriminately would be in violation of the terms and conditions of the grant."

"Ah . . ." Harry was fairly certain the government that had generously supplied the grant would be more than happy to see that Elaina Gomez receive the novel. Arguing, however, would do him no good.

"I hope you understand that by bending the rules, you have, within a few short days, put our entire community college in serious jeopardy of receiving future funding."

Harry clenched his teeth to keep from arguing. How ridiculous; Dr. Conceito was overreacting. What a small-minded man. Celeste had warned him, and without even trying, Harry had already waded waist-deep in trouble.

"I deeply regret causing any problems," Harry said, as contritely as he could manage. The pompous so-and-so. How he wished he could give this man what he so richly deserved. It took every shred of control Harry possessed to sit and do nothing. It hit him then: So this was what anger felt like. He was experiencing anger for the first time. Anger and frustration. The emotions were so powerful they nearly overwhelmed him.

Dr. Conceito continued. "I want to be sure nothing like this will ever happen again."

"It won't," Harry managed to assure him.

"Good." He dismissed Harry with a wave of his hand. That smile that was no smile was back in place. "And you'll be at the choral performance this evening."

"I'll be there," Harry murmured, more than eager to leave the president's office before he said or did something to get himself dismissed entirely.

He was halfway to the door when Dr. Conceito stopped him. "I have my eye on you, Mills. You're a troublemaker, and if this sort of behavior continues, you won't last long on this campus."

Harry clenched his fists. "I understand."

Dr. Conceito's assistant sent him a sympathetic look as he left the office. He didn't have a destination in mind, other than to escape. Passing the Hub, he headed toward his classroom and was stopped by a familiar voice.

"Harry."

Celeste stood outside the cafeteria area, sipping a hot drink from one of the coffee bar's cups. She wore a bright turquoise scarf, which was wrapped multiple times around her neck over a red coat.

Harry paused.

"What did I tell you?" she asked softly, then took a sip. Steam rose from her cup as she met his gaze above the rim.

"Stay away from Dr. Conceito. But I blew it, and now Dr. Conceito claims he's got his eye on me."

"He does," Celeste agreed, "but that's inevitable."

"It is?"

"The man has his demons, Harry, and your light clashes with his darkness."

What she said made sense. "He wants to get rid of me."

"Don't worry, we've got you covered."

"We?"

Celeste grinned. "You don't honestly believe God would send you on your first earthly assignment without backup, do you?"

Harry grinned. He should have realized he was being looked after. "I was angry." The power of the emotion surprised him.

"Eventually you'll learn to deal with these human feelings. It takes time," Celeste told him. "Emotions are what makes becoming friends with Michelle Heath so dangerous."

"How's that?"

The barista's gaze showed sympathy. "You can't become romantically involved with her, Harry. She's a beautiful woman and she's taken a liking to you."

He understood far too well; he'd taken a liking to the French teacher, too. "I fully intend to avoid her."

"What about the concert?" Celeste asked.

"When the time comes, I'll find a way to sit elsewhere." Harry wasn't worried. It shouldn't be difficult.

"How are matters with Addie Folsom progressing?" Celeste asked next.

Ah yes, his assignment. "She was in class on Wednesday but seemed distracted."

"Do you know why?"

"Not completely," he was forced to admit. "Erich fell, you know, and needed her help."

"And?"

"Addie willingly came to his aid." The young woman had made several strides in the right direction, and Harry was proud of her. "I'm still not sure what she is meant to learn from him, but she is evolving, conducting herself more maturely—and with more generosity—and that can't be bad."

"What happened after she helped him?"

This was the best part. "They started talking and realized their differences, despite everything, weren't all that great. It's a start. I think Erich is seeing her in an entirely different light."

"And Addie? Has her opinion of Erich changed, too?"

Harry grinned and nodded. "I believe it has."

Celeste looked pleased. "This is excellent news. Humans tend to build walls when they should be opening doors."

Harry regarded his mentor in a fresh light. "That sounded almost poetic."

"Thank you." She sipped her drink and then looked him square in the eye. "Now for the big question. Is Addie ready?"

Harry's thoughts felt as though they were caught up in a tornado, whirling around inside his head. *Ready for what?* He decided to wing it, no pun intended. "I think so."

"Good, because it won't be long now before Ashley arrives."

Chapter Nine

It was a couple days after her late-night summons for help, and Addie woke with her mind full of Erich. She pushed thoughts of him from her head and reminded herself that she hadn't finished reading the next fifty pages of *A Christmas Carol*.

Since helping Erich off the floor, their relationship had made a dramatic shift. Whereas before she was constantly on guard and tense around him, since his fall they'd found reasons to work together and even joke with each other. Never in all her life had Addie expected to laugh with Erich Simmons instead of at him or vice versa. This was completely unfamiliar territory. Even now she wasn't entirely sure she could or should trust him. He was everything she'd spent the last six years trying not to be. But then, look where that had gotten her. Nowhere, to be precise.

For breakfast, Addie blended fruit and protein powder along with milk and ice cubes into a frothy mixture that would be easy for Erich to drink without the use of his hands. This was the second morning she had mixed up the drink. She hoped the extra protein would give him badly needed strength. He'd seemed to enjoy it the day before, weakened as he was from all his efforts to get up off the floor.

Inhaling a calming breath, she put on her coat and carried the glass over to his house, letting herself in after a polite knock.

"Come in," he called, just as she came through the door.

As she expected, he'd spent the night in the recliner and was awake.

"Morning," she said, with a bit of uncertainty, holding on to the glass with both hands. Her heartbeat felt like a pogo stick pounding against her chest.

The evening before, they'd watched *Jeopardy!* together and then a movie. It'd been almost midnight before she'd gone to bed, and here she was again first thing in the morning. Given how incapacitated he was and that it was her job to care for him, that seemed appropriate. But she was unsure he would welcome her company so soon, so she waited a few seconds before moving into the living room.

"Morning," he said, and avoided eye contact.

That said a great deal. He, too, was at odds over all the time they'd spent together in the last couple days. She was fairly certain he was as uncomfortable about this shift in their relationship as she was.

"I made your breakfast," she said, stating the obvious, with the glass in her hand.

"I appreciate it."

She brought it over and set it down on the side table with a straw, and then stepped back awkwardly.

She waited, unsure what to do or say next, if anything.

The silence felt both heavy and bleak.

"Did you sleep well?" she asked, hoping to make polite conversation.

He glanced up and nodded. "Better than the night before. How about you?"

"Okay." Actually, she'd had a difficult time falling asleep, and when she did, her dreams had been filled with nightmares. She'd even dreamed of that time from her childhood when Erich handed her a dead worm and insisted she eat it if she wanted access to the fort he'd built with Jerry and Karl.

Silence again.

"Can I get you anything more?" she asked, eager now to be on her way.

VISIT THE SET
of
Mr. Miracle

A Hallmark Channel
Original Movie

The Heart of TV

*P*roduction begins!

A heartfelt moment between Addie and her mother.

$\mathcal{I}$t looks like Celeste has found a new friend!

$\mathcal{A}$ddie and Erich start to reconnect after not seeing each other since high school.

Here's Mr. Miracle himself, played by Rob Morrow.

Rob Morrow and Michelle Harrison play angels on a mission.

*B*ritt Irvin as Addie makes a mess baking cookies!

Following Harry's advice, Addie gains some perspective from reading *A Christmas Carol.*

PHOTOGRAPHS: KATIE YU

Britt Irvin and Andrew Francis have a fun moment on set.

Mr. Miracle has worked his magic!

Photo: Dane Gregory Meyer

Happy Holidays
from Debbie!

DebbieMacomber.com

"No. I'll be fine."

"Okay." There didn't seem to be anything else to say. Clearly, they were both uncomfortable with each other now, uncertain and hesitant. Although they'd lived next door to each other nearly all their lives, she realized that basically they were still little more than strangers.

His phone buzzed, indicating he had received a text. He read it and then glanced up at Addie. "Do you remember Carrie Hoffert?"

"Of course." They'd attended high school together. Carrie had been a homecoming princess and the leader of cheer squad.

"She's Carrie Welsh now. She heard about the car crash and wants to stop by."

Earlier, Erich had made it clear he wasn't in the mood for visitors. "How do you feel about that?"

He shrugged. "Okay, I guess. Carrie and I attended the University of Washington at the same time. Her husband and I work together at Boeing."

In other words, Carrie probably knew Ashley. That might prove interesting.

After chatting a few minutes more, Addie returned to the house and settled down to finish her reading assignment. To her surprise, the pages of Dickens's Christmas tale went rather quickly. It wasn't as if Addie didn't know what to expect in the story line; it was probably the most well known and loved of Dickens's novels. But even knowing the plot, she still found herself caught up in the characters and turning pages as eagerly as she would have if she hadn't known what would happen next. She looked forward to the classroom discussion and to hearing the reactions of her fellow classmates, especially Danny. He seemed to have a unique view of life in general.

The sound of a car door closing alerted Addie to a visitor. This was about the time the visiting nurse usually arrived, but it could be Carrie, too. Standing, Addie looked out the dining room window, which offered her the best view of the Simmonses' house.

Only it wasn't the visiting nurse, and it wasn't Carrie, either. The tall, thin, fashionably dressed woman in skinny jeans could only be the beautiful Ashley. She walked up the path to the front door as if she owned the street. She paused only long enough to flip her long, blond, perfectly styled hair off one shoulder before she rang the doorbell.

Unable to look away, Addie watched as Ashley let herself into the house. Addie wasn't sure how long she remained at the window. Her chest started to hurt, and after a moment she realized she'd been holding her breath.

Apparently, Erich and Ashley were enjoying a lengthy conversation, because Ashley stayed inside the house for a good long while. Addie checked her watch and could have sworn far more than only ten minutes had passed. It felt more like an hour. This was crazy. What did she care if Erich reunited with his ex?

Forcing herself away from the window, she returned to the kitchen and placed dirty dishes in the dishwasher. When she finished, she hurried back to the dining room window. Ashley's car was still there.

For reasons Addie didn't want to examine, she was angry, pacing the house, walking aimlessly from room to room. By the sheer force of her will she refused to look out the window again.

Thirty minutes passed, and when she could stand it no longer, Addie looked again. The other woman's car was gone. While she stood at the window, another vehicle pulled in to the same space so recently vacated.

It wasn't the nurse then, either, unless Carrie Hoffert Welsh had taken up a medical profession. She didn't look like any nurse Addie had ever seen, dressed in a red hooded coat. It seemed Erich had an entire parade of women at his beck and call.

Addie watched as Carrie stood on the front porch with a basket draped over her arm. She suspected Little Red Riding Hood had lovingly prepared chicken soup for poor, disabled Erich.

Addie pulled herself up short. Oh crap, she sounded as though she was jealous. Of Ashley and Carrie? Unbelievable! She refused to even consider such a thing.

Determined to push aside her less-than-kind thoughts, Addie returned to her book, although her thoughts wandered away from the page. More than once she had to force herself to refocus.

About fifteen minutes later her doorbell rang. She was surprised to find Carrie on the other side of the door.

"Carrie," she said, as though it was a complete shock to see the girl from her high school class. Well, actually, it was a surprise to see her at the door. "Come in, please." She invited her into the house.

"Addie, hello. It's been way too long; you look great." Carrie's smile was warm and sincere.

"You, too," she managed, and genuinely meant it. She remembered Carrie being a good, caring person, and it wouldn't surprise her if Erich had maintained their friendship through high school and college.

"Dave told me about Erich's accident, and so I brought him some Christmas cookies. He told me you're looking after him, and I thought I'd just pop over to say hi—it's been a long time. I hear you are helping so your two mothers can go on a cruise. That's really thoughtful of you, Addie. How's he holding up?"

Before Addie could answer, Carrie continued, "He put on a brave front, but I could see this is difficult for him."

It'd be difficult for anyone, but Addie refrained from saying so. "Erich is doing about as well as can be expected," she said.

"It's really kind of you to help him and give your mother and his the opportunity to travel."

"It's the least I can do." It wasn't necessary to explain that it'd taken a gentle shove from a barista and a classic-literature instructor to convince her to take on the task. Needless to say, the only reason she'd agreed was for her mother's sake. She hadn't exactly gone into this with a pristine attitude.

"If I'd been thinking, I could have brought Erich chicken soup instead of cookies," Carrie continued.

"You're the thoughtful one," Addie said. "I'm sure he'll enjoy the cookies."

"I hope so. It's good to see you, Addie. Erich tells me you're in school. That's great. I better get to work or I'll be late. Merry Christmas," she said, and started for the door.

"Merry Christmas," Addie returned.

Addie's spirits lifted as she walked Carrie to the front door and watched her drive away.

She waited until the visiting nurse had come and gone before she stopped by Erich's again. It was close enough to noon to think about preparing his lunch. She heated up to-mato soup out of a can and brought it over to him, along with a grilled cheese sandwich.

She knocked once and then let herself into the house. Erich had changed clothes and shaved, or rather been shaved. He looked good, better than she could remember seeing him since the car accident. The swelling had gone down in his eye and the bruises were fading. The color was back in his face and there was a spark in his eyes. No doubt the beautiful Ashley was responsible for that.

"I see you've had a busy morning," she said, putting on her best candy-striper smile. She didn't intend to bring up Ashley, but hoped he'd volunteer the information.

"Yeah." He didn't elaborate.

"I brought your lunch."

"So I see."

She set the cup and plate down and made a conscious effort not to leap back the way she had earlier. If he no-ticed, he didn't say anything. She stared at him intently, waiting. Nothing.

He frowned slightly. "What did you do this morning?"

She couldn't very well admit she'd been glued to the window, watching his house. "I read."

He seemed in a much better mood than earlier. And why not? Most likely his romance with Ashley had shifted to the on-again stage. It was on the tip of her tongue to ask him about his visitors, but she refused to do it. No way did she want Erich knowing she'd been watching the house.

"I'm going out this afternoon," she told him.

"Oh?"

If he wanted to keep secrets, then she could as well. There was no need to tell him she planned to attend the Christmas concert at the community college. Leave him guessing. "I'm meeting a couple guys from my class." A slight exaggeration. She was bound to run into Danny, who'd mentioned he'd be at the concert. And there was sure to be one or two others attending.

Some of the sparkle left his eyes. "Will you stop by later, then?"

She shrugged as if it was no big deal. "If you'd like."

"Sure, why not? It gets boring just sitting here for hours on end."

He seemed to be making sure she knew he wanted her company only out of sheer desperation. He wasn't interested in her, which was perfectly fine by Addie, seeing that she had no romantic interest in him, either.

"See you later," she said, eager to be on her way.

"See you," he called after her.

Addie couldn't get away from him fast enough. Once back at her own home, the same restlessness that had plagued her earlier returned. She showered, did a bit more housework, and then drove over to the college. She was an hour early for the concert. With time to kill, she stopped in at the Hub and ordered a latte before she remembered that she'd forgotten to eat lunch. No wonder she was hungry. The barista was the same one she'd spoken to earlier.

"I was hoping you'd be back," Celeste said, as Addie slid onto the stool. "What did you decide to do about your neighbor?"

Addie was reluctant to talk about Erich, but at the same time she needed a sounding board. "I took your advice."

"So how's it going?" The other woman busied herself with brewing the latte while she spoke.

Addie hesitated and then shrugged. "All right, I guess."

"Problems?" she asked, as she set the drink on the counter in front of Addie.

Taking the cash out of her purse, she considered her answer. She wanted to talk, but wasn't sure what to say, finally settling on "Not really."

Celeste braced her hands against the counter. "Then why do you look like you've lost your best friend?"

"Do I?" She had no clue she was this readable.

"Is he as disagreeable as you remember?"

Addie shook her head. "Not really . . . we actually seem to be getting along. I guess I was more comfortable when I couldn't stand the sight of him."

"Really?" Celeste looked surprised.

These questions unnerved Addie. "I . . . don't know. I'm sort of waiting for him to say something that will bring us back to the way things used to be. I'm more comfortable with that, and I think he is, too."

"Change is hard," the barista commented, as another student approached the stand and placed an order.

Celeste made a second latte and continued to chat with Addie as she worked. "Isn't that what Dickens's story is about?" she asked.

Addie hadn't thought of it in that way, but she had to agree. *A Christmas Carol* was indeed about change. Like her, Scrooge acknowledged the mistakes he'd made and realized he'd been given a second chance. The same way she'd been handed this gift of a second chance with education . . . and with Erich. She wasn't the only one, she realized. Danny, who'd served time, had been given a second chance as well, and Andrew Fairfax, the veteran who'd come to class with the service dog named Tommy.

Addie's thoughts were full of her short conversation with Celeste as she headed toward the concert hall. She saw Danny going into the building where their classroom was. Out of curiosity, she followed him inside, but once she was through the doors, she didn't see him. She headed down the hall toward their classroom.

The janitor was inside, but he didn't see her as he picked

up the garbage can. Instead of emptying it, he rifled through the can and took out a couple of wadded-up pieces of paper and read them.

Addie scooted back from the doorway, not wanting him to know what she'd seen. She had to wonder what he thought he'd find.

Addie was standing outside the classroom when Danny exited the men's room. He saw her and looked surprised.

"Hi, there! You going to the concert?" she asked.

"I thought I might. You?"

"Yeah. Mind if I walk over with you?"

"Sure thing." Danny was more than accommodating. "Did you finish the reading assignment yet?" he asked.

She nodded. "You?"

"Yeah. You kind of have to hate Scrooge. He was a greedy, mean SOB. Making Bob Cratchit work on Christmas." A thoughtful frown came over him and he lowered his voice and said, "I had a job once."

Once being the operative word, Addie realized.

"I would have worked on Christmas, but they closed the restaurant for the holiday."

"What was the job?"

He shrugged as if to tell her it was no big deal. Although from his body language, she felt it might have been.

"It was a barbecue place. I bused tables. My crew dissed

me when they saw me wearin' an apron, so I bailed. Big mistake."

"We all make mistakes, Danny. Big and small. But you don't have to let them define you forever. And isn't that what this book is about?"

"I thought it was about ghosts. Freaky!"

"Well, it is about ghosts and a whole lot more, don't you think?"

"She's right," Harry Mills said, walking up and joining them, heading toward Massey Hall.

Because she'd been involved in conversation, Addie hadn't realized anyone was behind them.

"I'm anxious to hear what you both think in class tomorrow," Harry said. "It seems like you're reading the story very thoughtfully."

When Addie had signed up for this course she'd been determined to do whatever it took to get through with a passing grade. She hadn't expected to enjoy it or even learn from it. Yet the novel they were studying was filled with life lessons that seemed to apply directly to her.

Chapter Ten

Harry waited until the very last minute to enter Massey Hall, where the choral group was about to make its Christmas presentation. It'd been his intention to arrive late. The later, the better.

He hadn't needed to make up an excuse. After speaking with Addie and Danny, he'd returned briefly to his classroom and been waylaid by the custodian.

"Mr. Mills," the janitor whispered, motioning him over. He leaned against the mop handle, which rested inside a large metal bucket.

Harry knew the man's name was Jonas from something Celeste had mentioned earlier, although he couldn't remember exactly what it was she'd told him. Human frailties could be downright frustrating. Memory being one of those.

"Yes," Harry said, as he approached the other man. "How can I help you?"

"You're new here, right?"

"I am," he said, and thrust out his hand. "Harry Mills."

The other man clasped his hand. "Jonas Spelling." He looked directly at Harry in an unsettling way as if measuring his words. "I heard you came from a teaching position in Oregon State Community College."

This was a gray area Celeste had told him was best to avoid. "I did."

The other man looked him over from head to foot as though Harry was in a police lineup and he was about to make a positive identification. "I have a brother who works at the same college where you taught. He knows everyone and he claims he's never heard of you."

Red lights started flashing right before Harry's eyes. He was not used to having to lie. "I'm sure if your brother checks the records, he'll find my name."

"Yes, yes, of course," Jonas said. "Anyway, that isn't the reason I wanted to talk to you." He lowered his voice as though afraid someone might be listening in on their conversation.

Harry made a point of glancing at his wrist, letting the

other man know he had commitments. Then, in a flash, Harry remembered what Celeste had told him. Jonas Spelling was a known snoop. Harry had to wonder how it was that he attracted all the oddballs.

"I won't keep you long," the janitor promised.

"I appreciate that. I have a concert to attend." He did his best to sound as official as Dr. Conceito.

"Yes, yes." The other man hesitated and looked down. "I have a couple concerns I thought you should know about."

"Concerns?"

"Yes." Again he lowered his voice and glanced over his shoulder. "It's about that war vet in your class. The one with the dog."

"Andrew?" Harry had done his best to draw the reticent student into the class discussion, without success. Andrew sat in the very last seat in the back of the room and kept his head lowered, avoiding eye contact.

"Didn't know his name," Jonas continued, whispering now.

"Is there a problem?"

"A potential one. I think the man might be mentally unstable."

Harry feigned surprise.

"Furthermore, the dog sheds hair. It isn't a good idea to be bringing a dog into a classroom."

"I disagree," Harry said. "I think this class is exactly where Andrew needs to be, and as for the dog, federal law allows service animals into classrooms. Even if I did have a problem with Tommy, and I don't, I couldn't do anything about it." *And wouldn't,* he added silently.

Jonas nodded as if he understood. "You're a kindhearted person, I can see that. Still, I thought you should be aware of the potential danger you and the class might be in. You never know about these returning veterans. They can go ballistic without warning."

"Thank you for your concern," Harry said pointedly, tamping down his irritation, "but I have everything under control."

The janitor leaned closer, causing the mop handle to sway toward Harry. "You don't need to worry. I've spoken to Brady Whitall, and he's keeping close tabs on the vet and the dog."

"The security guard?" This didn't bode well.

"Yes. Brady will keep a close eye on Andrew and on that felon."

"Felon? What felon?"

"The one on parole. Watch him closely; he's not to be trusted. He could rob you blind before you know what he's doing. He's a troublemaker if ever there was one."

Rather than argue, Harry made his excuses and hurried toward the performance center. As he walked, he tried to digest the conversation. This was a shock. Harry hadn't expected Earth to be filled with such mean-spirited people.

Once inside the performance center, it didn't take Harry long to spot Michelle. She sat near the front of the auditorium, close to the aisle. She'd placed her winter coat over the back of the seat next to her, the one she'd purposely saved for him, Harry realized. She glanced over her shoulder a couple times while he stood out of view. He was determined to follow Celeste's advice and stay away. Michelle was dangerous. Human, beautiful, single, and looking . . .

Harry waited until Michelle turned back around before he ducked into the first available seat and hunkered down. To his dismay, she stood as though to come in search of him. A trapped feeling settled over him. Harry had to do something, and quickly. He closed his eyes and did what was necessary. This was an emergency situation: Under normal circumstances, he wouldn't use his heavenly powers, but he had no other choice.

After a thorough search of the area, Michelle reluctantly returned to her seat. Harry released a sigh of relief.

Then Michelle hesitated and her head came slightly back as she realized the chair she'd saved for him had vanished. The person who had been two seats over was now sitting directly next to her. She glanced down the row but seemed to realize that something was strange. It wasn't as if her neighbor had moved, because there were no other empty seats. And no one else had come into the row. The chair had simply disappeared. She asked the person sitting directly behind her, apparently a friend, who shook her head and shrugged. With even more reluctance, she removed her jacket and reclaimed her seat.

Everything would be fine as long as Celeste didn't catch wind of what he'd done. He knew this was not really within parameters.

It wasn't until Harry relaxed that he realized he'd sat down next to Addie Folsom.

She smiled over at him and he smiled back. Actually, this had worked out amazingly well. He'd hoped to have a friendly chat with her and catch up on the progress she'd made with her neighbor. He had recently had a major insight. He'd become convinced that whatever Addie and Erich had to learn from each other might involve them falling in love. And he even thought the seeds were already there and taking root. Addie had had a crush on Erich in her early teens, and he suspected her feelings had never really changed.

"Hello, Addie," he said. "When I heard you and Danny talking earlier, I was impressed—you have a keen grasp of Dickens and this novel."

A smile flickered in and out of her eyes as though she was pleased by the compliment but unwilling to show it. "Thank you."

"Your progress has been excellent; I'm eager to read the written assignment when you turn it in."

It surprised him that his compliments caused her to blush. She didn't seem like a woman who blushed easily. As an angel, he wasn't really familiar firsthand with the feelings that caused blushing, but he was starting to pride himself on his insight into human nature. He changed the subject to help her out. "I understand you decided to look after your neighbor."

She frowned and looked away. "Yes."

He wanted to ask what had happened, but clearly he couldn't. He wondered if Ashley had made an appearance, just as Celeste had said she would. It didn't seem like matters had smoothed themselves out, either, whatever had happened. He felt the need to reassure her without making mention of anything specific. Weighing his words carefully, he leaned over and whispered in a conspiratorial manner, "You don't need to worry. I realize you harbor deep feelings for your neighbor."

Addie jerked away as if he'd struck her. "You've got to be kidding! Erich and me? No way. I can't imagine what ever gave you that idea."

"Ah . . . ah sorry, I thought . . ."

"You thought wrong," she snapped, and crossed her arms tightly across her chest.

"Clearly I made a mistake." Harry backpedaled as if in training for the Tour de France.

"You sure did." She glared at him as if to state she had nothing more to say on the subject.

Another blunder. Harry didn't understand. He knew in his heart that what he said was true; Addie did have feelings for Erich at one time, and he was fairly certain she still did. This is what made humans so difficult to understand. Addie did care for Erich, and yet she wasn't willing to admit it. He shouldn't have gotten ahead of himself.

Nothing could compare to the music he'd heard in heaven, but the concert had been lovely, the music quite good. When the presentation ended, there was a large round of applause.

Before Michelle could find him, Harry quickly left the performance center. He sought Celeste at the Hub. She was just getting off work and left with him so they could talk privately.

"So how'd your day go?" she asked, as they walked side by side.

Harry held his hands behind his back as he matched his steps with hers. He knew this was a rhetorical question, as she knew very well his day had been a challenge from the moment he'd set foot on campus. He was walking on eggshells after his meeting with President Conceito.

"Better, I hope." No need to try to fool Celeste. "I'm doing everything within my power to avoid making another mistake."

"You're learning." The words were devoid of censure. "The adjustment from heaven to Earth takes time. You're bound to make errors in judgment until you find your footing."

"I am? I mean . . ." He bit off the rest of what he'd intended to say, for fear anything he said would be digging himself deeper into a hole from which he couldn't escape.

"I understand you sat next to Addie at the concert and the two of you were able to talk."

She would bring that up. "We had a short conversation." Short because Addie had been quick to cut him off. She'd buried her face in the program flyer, letting him know she had nothing more to say.

"She's upset that Ashley stopped by." It was a statement of fact rather than a question.

"Apparently so." The less he said, the better.

"Did Addie mention what happened?"

Harry felt bad for Addie, who didn't seem to recognize her own feelings for Erich. "She didn't say, but she was unwilling to discuss it with me."

Celeste considered his words, then suggested, "Why don't we check out the situation for ourselves?"

"You mean now?"

His mentor smiled at him. "Don't look so worried. This won't be an inquisition. We'll take a nice stroll in their neighborhood just as we have before and check out the two houses."

"Ah, sure. Good idea."

Addie's home was several miles from campus, but they had walked only a few minutes when they turned the corner to Addie and Erich's street.

They stood across the street, again hidden against the backdrop of fir trees. The neighborhood was bright, with colored lights strung across rooflines and tree trunks, and with the chill in the air it was beginning to feel very festive. It was a beautiful clear night, and the stars sparkled above the lights sparkling below.

"Both houses are lit up inside, so both Addie and Erich seem to be home," Celeste said, as she motioned toward the two houses.

"I see Addie," Harry said, a bit excited. His young charge stood in the dining room, holding back the drape and looking out the window at Erich's home.

"Yes, I see her. She's wondering if she should check on him before she turns in for the night."

Harry didn't ask how Celeste knew what the other woman was thinking.

"She brought him dinner right after the concert, but she barely said a word to him."

"I was afraid something like that might happen," Harry said. He had a feeling that matters had taken a turn south in their relationship and that he might have inadvertently contributed to that.

Celeste sent him a meaningful look. "Apparently, your remarks shook her up a bit, not to mention Ashley's visit earlier. Addie was in and out of the house within minutes. Conversation was kept at a minimum."

"I was only trying to speed matters along," Harry murmured. He wanted Addie to recognize her feelings for Erich, but now he realized his comments had done more harm than good.

"Addie's miserable," Celeste said, sighing.

"What's Erich thinking?" Harry asked. If she was privy to Addie's thoughts, she could probably read Erich's as well.

Celeste moved slightly and looked up at the full moon that shed golden light across the lush green landscape. "He's confused. While Addie was at the concert, he painstakingly changed clothes and anxiously awaited her return. He was going to suggest she stay and watch television with him."

This was going from bad to worse. Harry felt guilty. "Any way to fix this?" he asked.

"Addie likes hot cocoa."

Harry wasn't sure what that had to do with anything.

"Erich does, too."

"And?" He needed a bit of direction. More than a hint, because he didn't have a clue what a hot drink had to do with the situation.

"You might plant the idea of Addie taking Erich a mug of hot cocoa."

"I can do that?" he asked, and then realized that he could. "I can do that!" he repeated emphatically. He shouldn't have forgotten. He had special powers he could use to help those in his classic-literature class.

Closing his eyes, Harry concentrated on placing the thought in Addie's mind.

When he opened his eyes, he saw that Addie remained standing in the dining room, looking out the window at Erich's house. "It didn't work," he said, feeling defeated.

"Don't be so sure."

"She hasn't moved."

Celeste smiled. "She's weighing her options. We can only suggest, Harry. Humans have the gift of free will. They have to make the decision themselves once we prayerfully urge them in one direction or another."

This wasn't new information. Yet Harry needed the reminder. He tried again and watched as Addie released the drape she'd held to one side and moved away.

"Where's she going?" Harry asked, anxious now.

Celeste glanced in his direction and smiled. "She's headed toward the kitchen."

Chapter Eleven

Addie released the drape and moved away from the dining room window that looked over the Simmonses' property. Her nerves were on edge. When delivering Erich's evening meal she'd been abrupt and short-tempered, eager to get in and out of the house with the least amount of fuss. It was on the tip of her tongue to make some derogatory comment about seeing Ashley, but she kept her nastiness to herself.

When she'd first arrived with his dinner, Erich had tried to engage her in conversation. She'd snapped at him about being extra-busy and hurried home.

Erich looked completely baffled by her behavior, and,

frankly, she didn't blame him. To this point, well, other than the first couple of meetings, they'd managed to be decent to each other. This evening she couldn't get away from him fast enough.

As soon as she was home, Addie regretted the way she'd acted. For the last two hours she'd paced the house, angry with herself. Finally, she'd settled in front of the dining room window, wondering what she should do now, if anything. It might well be that her gruff behavior had destroyed the fragile peace between them.

Because she was upset, Addie hadn't eaten dinner. She had no appetite, but felt she needed something in her stomach to stop the growling. Searching the kitchen cupboard, she found a tin of cocoa mix. For an elongated moment all she did was stare at it. Erich and her brother used to love drinking hot cocoa after one of their epic snowball fights whenever there was a rare Seattle snowstorm. It stung briefly to remember how the boys wouldn't let her join in their fun. Cocoa would make a nice peace offering, she decided.

Before she could talk herself out of it, Addie made them each a cup, carefully heating the milk and stirring in the cocoa. Then she carried two steaming mugs across the yard. Precariously holding the mugs in one hand, she knocked on the front door with the other and then nervously let herself into the house.

Erich was up and about. Surprise showed in his eyes when he realized it was her. The instant he saw her, he scowled.

"What's that? Poisoned cocoa?" he asked.

Despite herself, Addie smiled. "No, it's a peace offering."

His head came slightly back as if he wasn't sure he should believe her. "Oh?" The question carried more than a hint of sarcasm.

"I'm here to apologize," she clarified.

His gaze narrowed suspiciously. "What's your problem? One minute you're warm and the next minute I get the Arctic freeze."

"I'll be honest. I happened to look out the dining room window earlier today and saw you had . . . company, and I'm not talking about Carrie. That was Ashley, wasn't it?"

He didn't answer right away, and when he did his voice dropped several decibels. "Yeah, that was Ashley."

"I can understand why you're attracted to her. She's . . . beautiful."

"She's heartless."

Addie didn't know what to make of that. "She seemed to stay quite a long time, and it seemed, you know, that the two of you might have decided to have another go at the relationship." Now that she'd started talking, she couldn't seem to stop. "Which is wonderful, if that's what you wanted. I mean, she's stunning and the two of you make quite a couple."

The air went still and flat between them. Addie continued to hold both mugs of hot chocolate and was beginning to feel foolish.

After a minute, Erich said, "My guess is, you didn't see Ashley leave."

"No." Mortified at her morbid curiosity, Addie had forced herself to move away from the window. When she'd looked again, Ashley's vehicle was gone.

"If you'd been watching, you would've noticed that we didn't exactly part on the best of terms. I told her before and I meant it: We're finished. She's out of my life."

"Oh." She wasn't sure what to say beyond that.

A huge grin appeared, dominating his face. "I'm beginning to think you were jealous."

Her denial was swift and adamant. "No, I wasn't."

"Au contraire."

"No," she insisted a second time. "I figured if the two of you were together again, Ashley wouldn't want me around, so I decided to stay away."

Grinning like the cat who'd found a bowl of cream, Erich slowly shook his head. "You were jealous."

"Fine, think what you like. Now do you want the cocoa or not?"

He cocked his head to one side, narrowing his gaze. "If

you'd decided to make yourself scarce, then why are you here now?"

She gestured with the mug. "Do you want this?"

"I want it."

His smile relaxed the lines in his forehead. "Thank you, Addie. I'm glad you're here."

"I am, too." She probably shouldn't be so willing to admit it.

"Would you like to hang for a while?" he asked.

She shrugged, struggling to hide her delight at his invitation. "I guess, sure."

"Watching *Jeopardy!* wasn't nearly as much fun without you."

"That's because your fancy degree guarantees you'll win."

"Nope," he countered. "Truth is, you're the only person my age who likes it as much as I do."

Setting the mugs down on the side table, Addie made herself comfortable in the recliner next to Erich. A classic Christmas movie, *The Bishop's Wife,* was playing.

"I remember seeing this as a kid and loving it," Addie admitted, as she reached for her drink and took a sip, keeping her gaze focused on the television screen. She immediately recognized the ice-skating scene. What she didn't tell Erich was that she used to close her eyes and try to imagine it was Erich who held her in his arms, guiding her across the ice. What fanciful dreams for a thirteen-year-old with her head in the clouds.

"It's one of my favorite movies, too," Erich said. "In fact, I've seen it two or three times. I certainly wouldn't mind seeing it again."

"You like *The Bishop's Wife*?"

He looked a bit embarrassed. "Don't tell anyone, but I'm sort of an old-movie buff. I'm especially fond of the movies from the late 1930s and 1940s. Weird, huh?"

"No, not at all. I am, too."

That opened the conversation to other classic movies they enjoyed, and Addie was surprised by how in tune their likes and dislikes were. It surprised and pleased her. She never would have guessed that their tastes in movies or anything else would be the same.

When the last scene played, Erich turned off the television. Addie couldn't think of a reason to linger; they'd both finished the hot cocoa and it was getting late. She started to get up.

"How's the reading for your class coming?" he asked, stopping her.

"Really good. I find it particularly interesting to hear the perspective of others in the class."

"What's your take on the novel?" he asked, and seemed genuinely interested.

"It's about change." Addie had gleaned that from the

text from the first, but now she was more sure than ever. "It could be my thoughts are leaning that way because of where I am in my own life. I'm making a big change, and that's the message I want and need to hear. Still, I think that's what Dickens was writing about."

"How so?"

"Look at Scrooge," she said, becoming more animated as she spoke. "Isn't he a great character? We haven't gotten to the part near the end of the book where he purchases a Christmas goose and delivers the gifts to Bob Cratchit and his family, but everyone already knows that's how the book ends. Scrooge went from that greedy, self-absorbed individual to a man who was giving and kind; it was an overnight transformation." She realized that kind of dramatic change didn't generally happen as quickly, but this was fiction and that was the way the story needed to be told.

Erich appeared to be weighing her comments carefully. "Do you believe this turnaround in Scrooge's personality lasted more than a few days or weeks?"

Addie had the feeling Erich was really asking about her and the steps she'd taken to change her own life. "I'd like to think it did. Scrooge recognized that he was wasting his life. He had nothing but his gold. It took three ghosts to show him that all the stuff in the world was incapable of bringing him happiness."

"Giving his money away did?"

"Scrooge didn't give away his gold," she corrected kindly, speaking off the cuff. "He gave of himself . . . and in doing so, he found what he'd wanted and needed all along."

"And what was that?"

"His heart. Until then, Scrooge had completely ignored his need for others, for relationships, and because he did, he became bitter and mean."

Erich's look became thoughtful. "It sounds to me like you have a good grasp of the story and the symbolism."

She relaxed back in the chair, more pleased than she wanted to admit by his compliment. "The thing is, I wonder if Dickens was thinking about symbolism when he wrote the story."

She went on, "This is pure conjecture on my part, but it seems to me that Dickens's purpose more than anything was to engage the reader in the tale. The symbolism was all part of the story, a natural by-product of a good storyteller." In sharing her insights, Addie voiced her thoughts aloud for the first time.

"I can't say what Dickens was thinking," Erich said.

"I can't, either," she was quick to tell him. "Like I said, my thoughts are speculation."

"Still," Erich continued, "you make a good point."

"Thanks." She hadn't meant to prattle on as if she were an expert on the subject, because heaven knew she wasn't. If anything, reading was her weak spot. But it would be interesting to hear what others in her class had to say about Scrooge.

They sat in companionable silence for a few moments, at ease with each other.

Erich glanced out the window. "Did you hear the weather reporter is forecasting snow over the next couple days?"

"Snow?" Addie hadn't paid much attention to the television since she'd gotten back from class. The prospect of snow thrilled her. "No, I didn't hear. I love it when it snows!"

"Don't look so happy. You know what it's like around Tacoma; everyone goes a little crazy."

While snow in the Pacific Northwest wasn't unusual, it wasn't the norm, either.

"But it's perfect for Christmas."

"Bah, humbug," Erich said, scowling again. "I may have just watched a classic holiday movie, but that doesn't mean I'm going to get all celebratory."

Oh yes, she'd forgotten, Erich wasn't a fan of the holidays. "I can't forget about Christmas, and I don't know how you can, either." Earlier Erich had said something negative, but she honestly couldn't believe it was possible to hate Christmas. "I hope you didn't actually mean you don't like celebrating Christmas. That was all a joke, right?"

"I meant every word. People go way overboard, spending money on things they can't afford, buying gifts for relatives they don't like who will either regift or return them."

Addie was aghast. "It seems to me you need a visit from three spirits yourself, Erich Simmons. Where's your goodwill-toward-men attitude? Your Christmas spirit?"

He snorted. "I must have left it behind in the car after the crash."

"That's what I was thinking." She got up from the chair. "It's clear to me you're going to need a bit of help getting into the true spirit of Christmas."

He rolled his eyes. "Spare me, please."

"I most certainly will not. You and I are stuck together for Christmas, and I refuse to let you put a damper on it."

"Stuck together?" he asked, adding inflection to his voice. "Is that supposed to be a compliment?"

"I didn't mean it like that."

"Then tell me, how did you mean it?"

"What I intended to say was . . ." She hesitated, unsure how best to explain herself. "Seeing that we're going to be spending the holiday together, I'd like to make it a happy occasion."

"Are you planning on cooking me a Christmas goose?" he asked, sarcastically.

"If that's what you want."

"Can you cook?"

She arched her brows and slowly shook her head. "It seems to me, you aren't aware that I spent the last several years working in a diner. A couple times I had to step in when the cook got sick and prepare the orders myself. So, yes, in a word, I'll be able to manage Christmas dinner, only . . ."

"Only what?" he asked, revealing how skeptical he was.

"Only I'm not sure I can cook for two. Every recipe I know is for twenty servings or more," she teased.

He grinned, and it was all Addie could do to tear her eyes away from him. It amazed her how good-looking he'd become . . . Well, he'd always been cute, but he was no longer a boy now, and it was different.

"I've never cooked a goose, but I'm willing to give it a try," she said, in an effort to distract herself, tearing her gaze away from Erich.

"I don't want anything special. As far as I'm concerned, Christmas is the same as any other day of the week. It's certainly nothing special to me."

Addie ignored him. "I think a small turkey, stuffing, cranberries, and a couple of side dishes will be perfect."

His look hardened, and when he spoke he raised his voice slightly. "Apparently, you didn't hear me."

"I did," she returned nonchalantly, "but I prefer to ignore what you had to say." She stood, and, placing her hands on her hips, she surveyed the room, doing a slow turn. "What we need is something tangible to put you in the spirit of the holidays."

Erich stood, too. "You aren't listening."

"A Christmas tree will put you in the holiday mood."

"I don't want a Christmas tree."

Addie ignored him again. "No worries. I don't need your help setting it up. I'm happy to do it myself."

"Not at my house you won't."

"I'm thinking a five-foot tree would be the perfect size." She studied the room, filling her mind with the vision of a fully decorated tree. That was a sure way to help the Grinch's heart grow three sizes. He might object now, but a decorated tree was just the ticket. He wouldn't be able to resist the holiday when every time he walked into the room he was confronted with the bright, twinkling lights of a Christmas tree.

"Addie, I'm serious. If you want to go through all the trouble of putting up a silly Christmas tree, do it at your own house and not here."

"I'm serious, too," she countered.

He grumbled under his breath. "Don't you have someplace else you need to be? Homework that needs to be read?"

"Are you saying you're sick of me?"

"As a matter of fact . . . I'm not, which sort of shocks me. Heaven knows I should be, with all this talk about Christmas."

Staring at him, she was struck anew at the deep shade of

blue his eyes were. How was it she'd never noticed that before?

"I find it unsettling how much I like hanging out with you," she said. "You're not half as bad as I remember."

"I was thinking the same thing," he said, joking back. "With the exception of you insisting on decorating a tree." He smiled then, and the mood lightened.

They stood there goofily, smiling at each other. Suddenly it seemed like the most natural thing in the world for him to kiss her. Addie wasn't sure who leaned toward whom first. It might well have been her.

Erich placed his wrists on top of her shoulders, the weight of his twin casts catching her by surprise. She tilted her head back to look up at him and closed her eyes as his mouth settled, warm and gentle, over hers. His lips were soft and his kiss stole her breath.

He released her quickly. As if they were two children who'd been caught doing something wrong, they stepped away from each other.

Erich spoke first. "Wow," he whispered. "That was wild!"

Addie smiled. "I know, right?"

He stepped closer and rested his forehead against her own. "Do you remember when we were eight?"

"Vaguely."

"You offered to pay me your allowance if I'd kiss you."

"I did?" Addie didn't remember any such thing. "Tell me you're making that up."

"Nope. I swear it's true."

"You didn't take me up on my offer, though, did you?"

Erich did a poor job of hiding his amusement. "Actually, as I remember it, I kicked you in the shins."

Addie's smile grew bigger. "That sounds like something you'd do."

"I was just thinking . . ."

"Yes?"

"I was just thinking," he repeated, "that I wouldn't be so willing to turn you down if you were to make that same offer again."

Chapter Twelve

The next morning Addie hardly knew what to think. Erich had kissed her. Actually, she might have kissed him! She couldn't remember who had done what. What did stick in her mind as she tossed and turned the night away was the absolute shock of it.

Erich?

Her?

Even as she sat on the edge of her bed, fighting off the last dregs of sleep, she didn't know how it'd happened. Nor could she figure out when things had changed or even what had changed. Clearly something drastic had.

Was it her?

Was it Erich?

She decided she'd blame Christmas. Perhaps this was his way of telling her his relationship with Ashley was completely over. That sort of made sense. It could be that they'd gotten caught up in the moment. Addie had always considered the holidays an extra-special time of year. Magic hung in the air, and people were gentler, kinder to one another. Differences were set aside, friendships deepened, and people in general were more charitable and happier.

That explained it, she decided. She would chalk the kiss up to Christmas.

Once she'd showered and dressed, Addie glanced out the dining room window toward Erich's house. Despite the early hour, she saw that his lights were on. Apparently he'd had trouble sleeping, too. She couldn't help speculating if he'd spent the night wondering about their kiss the way she had.

Maybe. Maybe not.

He'd probably brushed the incident aside and had completely forgotten it'd happened.

Seeing that he was awake and she was awake, Addie cooked him a breakfast of scrambled eggs plus toast and carried the meal from her house to his.

As was her habit, she knocked once and let herself in. Erich wasn't in the living room the way she'd expected. Standing just inside the entry, she called out for him.

"Erich?"

"In the kitchen." His voice came from the far end of the house.

He moved about considerably better now, she noticed. After several days sitting and sleeping in the recliner, she suspected he was thoroughly sick of remaining in the same position for hours on end, which gave her an idea.

"I brought you breakfast."

"Another protein drink?" he asked.

"No, eggs this morning."

She found him sitting at the kitchen table with the morning newspaper spread out across the surface. He was able to use his fingers more and more.

"Eggs." His eyes lit up.

"With cheese and chives."

He looked impressed. "Wow, you can actually cook."

Amused, she tossed him a dirty look, then set the plate down in front of him. "Do you want coffee?"

"Please."

Addie brewed him a cup and then made one for herself. When she finished she carried both mugs to the table and sat down across from him.

To this point, Addie had served him finger food or thin soups that he could drink through a straw. It pleased her to note that he was able to manage a fork. It wasn't easy or pretty, but he'd become adept enough to get the food to his mouth. It was evident that the effort taxed his patience, though.

"I have a question," she said, leaning slightly forward as she placed her elbows on the table. She could be opening a hornet's nest, but curiosity had won out and she couldn't stop herself.

He looked up. "Okay."

"Did we . . . you and I actually kiss last night?"

He paused and considered the question. "I seem to remember that we did."

"Didn't you find that just a little bit odd? You and me . . . kissing?"

Once more he mulled over her question, letting the fork dangle above his plate, holding it between his fingers. "I'd say it was more surprising than it was odd."

Addie didn't see it that way. "I found it shocking."

He held her gaze and studied her as though curious. "Do you always analyze a kiss this way?"

"Not before now."

"So I'm the first?"

"Yes."

He frowned slightly. "Should I take that as a compliment or insult?"

The question gave her pause. "I don't know. How do you feel about it?"

"Kissing you or how I felt afterward?" he asked.

She wasn't sure. "Both, I guess. You didn't plan it, did you?"

"Hardly. At the time it seemed the thing to do. I don't regret it, if you're looking for an apology." He set the fork down and pierced her with a single look. "What are you thinking?"

"I don't know yet. I think I probably should regret it, but I don't."

He grinned then, as if he found this discussion highly amusing.

"I'd like for the two of us to go out today," she said, speaking impulsively.

"And do what?"

"Just walk. You need the fresh air."

"Really?"

"Yes. It will do you good. You've been cooped up in this house far too long. You're up and about now and looking more like yourself every day. We don't need to go far."

"Not interested."

"Erich, don't be difficult. It'll be good for you."

He exhaled and leaned back in his chair. "I have the distinct feeling you're going to badger me until you get what you want."

"I won't badger you."

"No, you'll probably torture me into submission."

If he expected her to pout and demand her own way, she was sure to disappoint him. "You make me sound heartless, and I assure you I'm not."

"It won't be easy getting me ready for this."

"I know."

"You'll need to help me with my shoes and my coat." He said this as if it would be enough to cause her to change her mind.

"I'll be happy to do that."

No more than a half hour later, Addie opened the front door and they stepped into the cold December air. The morning was crisp, and the frost crunched beneath her feet as she stepped onto the lawn. The sky had clouded up to a shade of battleship gray.

Erich's gaze followed hers as he carefully moved down the three short steps leading off the porch. "If I could, I'd hold your hand."

"Ah, that's sweet," she said, and slipped an arm around his elbow, wanting to be sure he was steady on his feet. "How are you feeling?"

"Not bad."

The park where they'd so often played as children was two blocks away. Addie thought they could walk there, rest a bit, and then return to the house. That would be an outing enough for one day.

Erich looked toward the low-lying clouds a second time. "It smells like snow."

She appreciatively sniffed the air and agreed. "It does."

"No class today? No Mr. Mills?"

"No, it's been canceled due to the threat of snow, although I wish there were classes. I'm surprised how much I like this class and the people I'm meeting, especially Danny and Andrew."

"Hey, have I got competition?" he joked. "Have you been kissing them, too?"

"No," she said, laughing. "Andrew's the war vet I mentioned earlier. The one with the service dog named Tommy."

"What about the other guy? Danny, was it?"

"Yes, Danny. He's this big, tough-looking guy who's like a huge puppy. It seems he's got a comment for just about everything Mr. Mills says. He's got a great attitude, although his personality is a bit quirky."

"Quirky?"

"You'll know what I mean when you meet him."

Erich slowed his steps to a crawl. "And just when am I going to meet this felon friend of yours?"

"At the Christmas party Mr. Mills mentioned in our last class. It's a potluck. Everyone is bringing something."

"And you want to bring me?"

"Yes."

"I think," Erich said pointedly, "when Mr. Mills suggested you bring something, he was referring to a dish to be shared with others, not a person."

"I know what he meant, and I am bringing food. In fact, I'm baking cookies."

"Can you explain why you want to drag me to your class party?"

Addie had hoped that by mentioning the invitation casually, Erich wouldn't make a big deal of it. "I want to include you. It'll be fun and you'll enjoy the outing."

He automatically shook his head. "Thanks anyway."

Addie couldn't hide her disappointment.

Using his index finger, he lifted her chin so their eyes could meet. The last time he'd looked at her with the same intensity had been right before they'd kissed. "I don't think you were listening when I mentioned how I feel about Christmas."

"I heard you, but I didn't like what you had to say." He didn't know it yet, but she fully intended on purchasing that Christmas tree and decorating it. Furthermore, she planned to set it up inside his house. Erich could ignore the holidays if he wished, but she was going to make it as hard as possible.

"Are you saying," he asked, skeptically, as they continued on their walk, "you were so overwhelmed by the emotional magnitude of our kiss that you completely lost track of our conversation?"

"If that's what you'd like to believe, then sure, why not?" She flashed him a brilliant smile, hoping to dazzle him with her charm and wit. All too soon she realized it hadn't worked.

"Addie, I hate to disappoint you, especially when we're getting along so well. I'm not interested in this friendly little class get-together. I don't want to think about Christmas. My goal is to get through the next few weeks as best I can while I'm in these casts and ignore everything else."

"It's just that I'd hoped you'd come."

"Why would you even want me there?" he probed.

"Because I think you'd enjoy it. Is it me you're looking to avoid or everything else?" she challenged.

"Listen," he said, stopping in the middle of the sidewalk and turning to face her. "I don't want to put a damper on your festive mood. Both my wrists are in casts. Even the simplest movements that everyone takes for granted are beyond me. I'm not up to celebrating much of anything. Can you leave it at that?"

As much as she would have liked him to attend the class potluck, she understood what he was saying. "Okay, got it."

His shoulders sagged. "Darn. I was sort of hoping you'd want to argue."

"You were?"

"Yes." He looked down and smiled at her. "Then we could kiss and make up."

"Are you looking for excuses to kiss me again?" she teased.

He lifted his thick eyebrows with the question. "You interested?"

"Could be."

They reached the park just about the time it started to snow. The flakes were heavy and thick.

"Stick out your tongue," Addie urged excitedly.

"What?"

"Don't you remember when we were kids, we used to catch snowflakes on our tongues?"

"The key phrase here is: *We were kids*. That's something kids do. Not adults."

"Erich. What's happened to you? When I knew you before, you were up for just about anything."

"The point is, I have two broken wrists," he returned in quick order. "This past week hasn't been fun, you know."

"I realize that, but it isn't enough of an excuse to be mad at the world."

"The person I'm mad at is the driver who slammed into my car at fifty miles an hour. I'm mad because I'm as helpless as a baby. And I'm mad because I'm being forced to use my vacation time and accumulated sick leave to sit around my mother's house and be treated like an infant. And I hate Christmas. Let's leave it at that."

That left her wondering if he was talking about something other than the accident that'd happened in his own life. His father hadn't died in December. Addie remembered getting word about his dad around Saint Patrick's Day, so it must have been in March.

The silence seemed to throb between them.

"Okay," she whispered. "Message received."

By unspoken agreement, they started walking back toward the house.

It was Erich who broke the silence. "Frankly, I think Scrooge got a bum rap."

"You do?"

"As far as I'm concerned, he had the right idea when it came to Christmas."

Chapter Thirteen

Humming a Christmas carol, Harry headed toward his class. His spirits were high. He'd managed to avoid Dr. Conceito for the last couple of days, and he found himself adjusting to the ways of Earth. Dealing with emotions continued to be a bit tricky, but he was getting there.

Two inches of snow had accumulated the day before, with more forecast for later in the afternoon. Harry loved snow. For several generations, youngsters had been making snow angels without ever suspecting where the original idea had come from. He smiled to himself as he crossed the campus. He was scheduled to meet with Celeste later and give his mentor an update on Addie Folsom.

The idea of his young charge taking Erich cocoa had worked famously. Harry knew the two had kissed and that Addie had managed to get Erich out of the house for a short walk the day before. Oh yes, matters were progressing nicely. Addie had shown vast improvement when it came to attitude. She truly had matured in the years she'd been away from her family. As for her relationship with Erich, it was too soon to tell. Still, Harry could see significant progress had been made. He couldn't take all the credit, he realized, but Celeste would be pleased.

In fact, Harry could hardly wait to tell Celeste about the kiss. She'd be thrilled. Two people who had never been able to tolerate the sight of each other were now . . . friends, with the potential for a whole lot more.

Harry was caught up in his thoughts and didn't notice until he reached his classroom that his room was the only one down the long hallway with the lights on.

He opened the door to his classroom and stopped cold.

Michelle Heath, the French teacher, was inside his room. She'd spread a red-and-white-checkered tablecloth on the floor, with one corner anchored by a wicker picnic basket. Two champagne glasses rested on top of the basket.

"Welcome, Harry," she whispered seductively.

His tongue felt like it was glued to the roof of his mouth. "Hi," he finally managed.

"I missed seeing you in Massey Hall at the performance." Her lips formed a soft pout. She sat on the table-cloth with her legs bent behind her and looked up at him with the most enticing smile he'd ever seen. His heart was doing jumping jacks inside his chest.

"I . . . know. All the seats were taken by the time I arrived." He remained frozen, standing in the doorway.

"Come in," she beckoned, motioning him by wiggling her fingers.

Harry felt his Adam's apple bob up and down in his throat. "What . . . about class?" His students would arrive any minute. He could only imagine what Dr. Conceito would think if he were to make a surprise visit to the room and find Harry sipping champagne with the French instructor when he was scheduled to be teaching class.

"Didn't you hear?" Michelle asked, her eyes rounding with surprise.

"Hear?"

"Classes have been canceled due to the snow."

"Ah . . . no one told me."

"It was announced earlier." She removed the champagne flutes from the top of the basket and opened it. She set aside the lid and reached inside to take out a cutting board, a long loaf of crusty French bread, a block of cheddar cheese, and a bottle of champagne. When Harry didn't immediately join her, she glanced up.

"No need to be shy, Harry. Come sit with me." She patted the space on the floor next to her.

His knees had turned to the consistency of gelatin.

"I'm going to need you to open the champagne bottle for me," she said, looking at him with wide blue eyes that seemed to say he was the strongest, most capable man she'd ever known.

"Um . . . okay." He came all the way into the classroom and took the bottle from her hand.

"Sit," she urged.

Harry sank to the ground. His hands trembled slightly as he removed the wire mesh from the top of the bottle and discarded it in the wastepaper basket that was close at hand. Then he remembered how Jonas, the custodian, often rummaged through the trash, and quickly retrieved it. He thrust it into his jacket pocket along with the foil. He was determined there would be no incriminating evidence left behind.

"My first husband was French," Michelle explained.

"Your first husband?"

Her eyes were round and sad. "I've been married twice."

"Oh."

"You know what they say," she said, looking up at him with a hopeful expression. "The third time is the charm."

Harry's Adam's apple did a complete lap. "Third time?"

"Yes, I don't want to be alone any longer."

He was in trouble here. Big, big trouble.

"But that isn't what I wanted to tell you," Michelle continued. "This is about the champagne. Pierre said there was a trick to opening bubbly. Instead of twisting the cork, one must gently turn the bottle."

She made it sound easy, but when he attempted to do it, Harry discovered it was anything but. He gripped the cork and, following her instructions, gently rotated the bottle.

"If you open it slowly and carefully, it shouldn't make a popping sound. In fact, Pierre said when properly opened, champagne should have the sigh of a contented woman."

It was only by sheer good fortune that Harry managed to save the bottle before it went crashing to the floor. *The sigh of a contented woman.*

Heaven hadn't prepared him for this!

Harry didn't have a clue what a woman's satisfied sigh meant, but whatever it was sounded dangerous.

All at once the cork shot from the bottle with a popping sound loud enough to send fire engines racing toward the building. Harry nearly fell backward with the shock of it.

Michelle, however, barely seemed to notice. "Shall I pour?" she asked, when Harry remained frozen, clinging to the bottle with both hands.

Unable to respond any other way, Harry nodded.

Celeste had warned him about Michelle, and here he was like a fly trapped in a spider's sticky web, hardly able to move and struggling valiantly. But not nearly valiantly enough. At this point, Harry found breathing difficult. His head was wandering into territory no angel should explore.

Harry needed help. And he needed it fast.

Then, when he least expected it, the classroom door flew open with such force it bounced against the wall. Brady Whitall leaped into the classroom in a crouched position with his weapon drawn. Both hands held on to the Taser gun, which was pointed directly at Michelle and Harry.

Michelle screamed.

So did Harry, who toppled the champagne bottle.

Brady stared at them long and hard before he blinked and lowered his weapon. "What's going on in here?"

With her hand pressed against her front, Michelle looked as if she was about to faint. Harry was feeling light-headed himself.

"A . . . picnic," Harry managed, although it was difficult to speak with his mouth so dry.

Michelle started to mop up the champagne. "Let me explain, Officer," she said. "Would you care to join us?"

———

By the time Harry was due to meet Celeste an hour later, he was an emotional mess. Once more he'd failed, and she was sure to reprimand him. With good reason. He had made a terrible error in judgment.

With his hands over his face, Harry sat in the vacant cafeteria at one of the tables. The kitchen staff was just finishing the cleanup when Elaina, the young single mother he'd met earlier, saw him. Right away she came over.

"Hello, Mr. Mills," she said in perfect English, smiling. "I'm happy to see you again."

"Hello," he whispered back.

She frowned. "You okay?"

He nodded. It would be too difficult to explain that he'd just looked down the barrel of a police weapon. Because they were both badly shaken, they'd drank the entire bottle of champagne. Michelle insisted it was exactly what they needed. Now Harry wasn't so sure.

"You don't look so good." The frown had turned into worry lines that creased her brow.

"I don't?" This didn't bode well. Celeste would know right away that he'd messed up. It would be a miracle if he was allowed to finish teaching the course. He wouldn't be surprised if she banished him from Earth, and he wouldn't blame her.

Elaina pressed her hand against his forehead. "No fever."

He smiled weakly and hiccupped.

Next she reached for his hand, and, looking at her watch, she checked his pulse. After a moment, her eyes widened with alarm. "Your heart is beating very fast."

No doubt. Hers would be, too, if she'd come face-to-face with RoboCop.

"I'm fine," he insisted, although he didn't feel the least bit well.

Celeste was finishing counting out her register and would be joining him in a matter of minutes.

"I'll bring you something to calm you," she said.

"No . . . no."

"Please. You have been so nice to me."

Harry couldn't very well refuse and so he smiled, agreeing. "You're very kind."

"I hurry back."

"No rush."

Elaina left him and trotted back into the kitchen. She wasn't gone more than a couple minutes. When she returned, she carried a mug of steaming water, which she set down on the table in front of Harry.

"Sip this," she instructed. "Don't swallow fast. You understand?"

Harry nodded. Tea leaves, or what he assumed must be tea leaves, covered the bottom of the mug.

"Sip," she said again.

"I'll sip," Harry promised.

"Medicine from my country," she whispered. "It will relax you."

Harry watched as she returned to the kitchen. From the look, this was some herbal concoction she kept on hand for emergencies. Some home remedy. He took his first sip and noticed that Elaina must have added a tablespoon of honey, because the tea had a sweet taste.

Celeste approached and Harry yawned. He didn't know what it was that Elaina had put in the tea, but whatever it was had a powerful calming effect on him. Maybe it was the champagne, because now he seemed to be having trouble holding up his head. He was tempted to fold his arms and rest his head on the tabletop.

He gave Celeste a huge smile and then yawned.

She frowned. "Harry? What are you drinking now?"

"Tea. Elaina gave it to me to calm my nerves after Brady Whitall threatened me with a gun."

Celeste slowly shook her head. "I was afraid something like this would happen."

"Not only me, but that beautiful French woman, too."

"Michelle Heath," Celeste supplied.

"Right. She isn't French . . . she just speaks it."

"She's a French teacher."

Harry nodded and held up his index finger. "It was all my fault. I accept full responsibility. No one told me what the sigh of a contented woman sounds like."

Celeste grabbed the back of the chair. "I think I better sit down."

"Good idea," Harry whispered. "Can you tell me about that? Because I can assure you there was no such lesson in heaven. No one explained about French teachers with champagne, either. Were you aware," he said, waving his finger, "there's a very particular way to open champagne? It's dangerous, I tell you. Dangerous."

"Yup," Celeste whispered, pulling out the chair, "I think it might be best if I sit down."

"You shouldn't hurry home," Harry pointed out. "It's snowing."

"Yes, I know."

"Classes were canceled."

"So I understand."

"Someone should have told me. It would have saved me from all this." He waved his hand in front of his face. "Is it hot in here or is it just me?"

"It's just you," she said kindly, and patted his hand. "I need you to tell me what transpired from your point of view. Start at the beginning."

"In the beginning, God created . . ."

"Not that beginning," she said, stopping him. "Start with the French teacher and the gun."

Harry's shoulders sagged and he covered his face with both hands. "I don't think you're going to like this."

"Probably not," she agreed. "Go back to Michelle and the champagne. And you drank the entire bottle. Oh Harry, you should know better."

"You're right, I should have resisted." He dropped his hands and then placed one against his forehead. He'd failed when he was convinced he wouldn't have any problems. But then, he hadn't known Earth had women as lovely as Michelle Heath and drinks that tasted as wonderful as French champagne.

He'd been sent to Earth to help humans. Now he was badly in need of heaven's help.

Chapter Fourteen

"Just what are you doing?" Erich demanded when Addie breathlessly opened the front door. "I thought you were supposed to be studying for class."

"What does it look like I'm doing?" she returned, shoulders heaving with the effort of carting the five-foot-long fir tree from her car up the sidewalk and into the Simmonses' house. "I'm planting a tree in your living room." Actually, Addie was pleased with herself. It'd taken some doing getting the Christmas tree home.

"I already told you: no tree."

Addie had barely managed to get the Christmas tree

through the front door, and already Erich was making noises. "Did you?" she asked, playing dumb.

"Take that ridiculous monstrosity to your house," he insisted, none too gently.

She ignored his protests and dragged the tree all the way inside his living room. Who knew a tree could be so heavy? She'd found one at the lot when she stopped off at the grocery store. It was snowing, and she simply couldn't resist. Erich had made his point, but Addie refused to accept it. It wouldn't be Christmas without one of the most important traditions.

When she happened to look his way, Addie noticed that Erich's face was tight with agitation. "It's perfectly fine if you want to put up a Christmas tree, but do it at your house and not mine."

"I would, except for one thing." She stood in the middle of the room with her hands on her hips. The tree lay on the floor in all its natural glory.

"I can hardly wait to hear this," he muttered, his words thick with sarcasm.

"You're the one in need of Christmas spirit, not me. I can't think of a better way to put you in the mood for the holidays." She hesitated. "Oh, and you might want to reconsider attending the holiday potluck with my class."

"No to both," he said, scowling.

She released a low sigh. Clearly her plan wasn't working, but she was too committed to change course now. "Okay, fine. Whatever. I'll give you an out on the potluck, but not the tree."

"I always knew you were stubborn, but this is over the top. Would it be too much to ask you to listen to reason? This is my home, and I don't want anything to do with Christmas. Can I make it any clearer than that?"

"Message received."

"But you're not listening."

"No." He was being a Scrooge, and she wasn't going to let it happen. "Be careful or those three spirits might just pay you an uncomfortable visit," she warned.

"I'd rather deal with them than one stubborn female."

Erich looked away. With effort, she stood the tree against the wall and paused to look around to decide where best to set it up. "I bought something else while I was shopping."

"Whatever it is, it's a waste," Erich grumbled.

"You'll have to decide that for yourself," she said, as she continued to survey the room for the perfect spot for the tree. Her choices were few, but if she moved some furniture around a bit . . .

He mumbled something else, but Addie was only half listening. She reached for a small sack and brought out a sprig of mistletoe. "A waste, you say?"

"Yes, I already told you . . ." He stopped mid-sentence. The look on his face was priceless, as if he was debating how to react. "Mistletoe?"

Addie tossed him a saucy smile. "Aha, just as I thought. You have no objection to certain aspects of Christmas."

Scowling, he refused to meet her gaze. "In the interest of compromise, keep the mistletoe, take back the tree."

"Sorry, no can do."

He mumbled something unpleasant under his breath.

"Complain all you want, Erich Simmons, but I refuse to allow you to ignore Christmas. It's not happening on my watch."

Erich tilted back his head and closed his eyes. "Why me, God? First I break both wrists and then you send me this stubborn woman who refuses to leave me be. Why? Why? Why?"

"God sent you exactly what you need," she said. Inwardly, she was pleased God had sent her, not that she'd admit it to Erich, especially when he was in this sour mood.

"Get rid of it," he returned.

"The mistletoe?"

He grumbled again and shrugged as if he didn't really care one way or the other. "You can keep that."

Addie was exhausted. This Christmas-tree business was hard labor. "My dad used to say I was stubborn. I would have thought you'd know that by now."

"Now, that's an understatement if ever there was one."

"Ah, come on, Erich, lighten up. A Christmas tree is exactly what we both need. Okay, maybe you don't, but I do," she countered. This was as much for her as for Erich.

"Okay, fine; have it your way."

"Your enthusiasm overwhelms me," she joked.

"If you're looking for enthusiasm, you'll need to search elsewhere." His face was tight and dark.

"What is it with you?" she demanded. He should at least appreciate the effort she'd made to bring a bit of cheer into his life. As a kid, she recalled that Erich had been as excited about Christmas as Jerry and she were. He might pin his bad attitude on the car accident, but there was more to it than that.

"My attitude is not changing," he said, "so you'd better get used to it."

She reached for her coat and headed toward the front door.

"Hey," he said, stopping her, "where are you going now?"

She paused in the entryway. "To my garage for the tree decorations."

"You're coming back?" The question sounded as if he wasn't sure he'd welcome her company.

"Would you rather I stay away?" She was only half-serious.

"It's tempting to say yes."

Addie grinned because she knew he didn't mean it.

For the next half hour, Addie hauled plastic containers from her garage to Erich's house. It was demanding work. Erich watched, his gaze following her movements, but he remained stubbornly silent. When she'd finished stacking the containers in the living room, she went directly into the kitchen.

"Now what are you doing?" he said, following her into the other room.

She opened and closed cupboard doors. "I'm looking for a pan to pop popcorn."

"You're hungry?"

She shouldn't need to explain. "In case you're unaware, it's impossible to decorate a Christmas tree properly without eating popcorn and listening to the appropriate music."

"What's wrong with microwave popcorn?"

It shocked her that he was unaware of the most basic Christmas traditions. "It's not the same. Real popcorn is popped on the stove."

"This is a joke, right?"

She glared at him with a look that would have melted kryptonite.

"Okay, okay, you're serious," he said and backed away. "I'm sorry I asked."

He returned to the other room and Addie was just as glad.

While he was out of sight, she set her phone on the kitchen counter and went into her playlist for her favorite Christmas songs, everything from Bing Crosby to Bruno Mars.

The popcorn smelled heavenly, and the scent of it soon swirled through the house. Addie filled a large bowl, brought it into the living room, and set it on the end table next to Erich.

He glanced at her, then the popcorn, and announced, "I'm going to my room."

"Have it your way." This disappointed Addie, but she refused to let him know it. The music played as she cheerfully strung the lights around the tree, stopping now and again to nibble on popcorn. It really tasted so much better popped the old-fashioned way.

She finished the lights and had started hanging the ornaments when Erich returned. He slumped down into his chair as if he expected her to make a derogatory comment. Instead she came over to the chair, leaned over, and kissed him, letting her mouth linger playfully over his for several breathtaking seconds. Then, without a word, she returned to the task at hand, placing the ornaments on the tree.

"You need a few more toward the left-hand side of the tree," Erich instructed, sounding breathless following their kiss.

Stepping back, Addie tilted her head to one side and then the other. "You're right."

"Everyone's a critic," he said, almost regretfully.

The last decoration was the angel for the top of the tree. Addie brought it out of the protective box and studied it. The angel's white dress had faded over the years and her wings weren't what they'd once been; still, she was beautiful to Addie because of all the memories associated with her.

"Dad bought this for Mom the first year they were married," she said, carefully cradling the figurine in her hands. "He always waited until Christmas Eve before he placed her on the tree. We'd attend church services and come home around nine or ten. Then Dad, with a great deal of ceremony, would put the angel on top of the tree."

"Traditions are important," Erich surprised her by commenting.

"They are. It's those memories that stay with us, that bond us as family. It's one of the reasons I made sure I was home nearly every Christmas. I couldn't imagine not baking cookies with Mom, or decorating the tree with my father. We might have argued a good portion of the time, but it would be unthinkable to give up that special time together because of our differences."

She'd finished with everything except the angel, which she tucked back into the box. Pushing the empty containers out of the way, she stepped back and then slowly smiled. "I don't care what you say, this is one truly beautiful Christmas tree."

He shrugged.

"Oh come on, Erich, admit it, this tree is gorgeous."

"I'll admit nothing of the sort."

"Twit." That was a name he'd called her as a kid, when she'd get upset with his teasing.

He grinned as if he, too, remembered the name-calling of their youth. "When do you intend to put up that mistletoe?"

"Soon. But I seem to remember kissing you only a few minutes ago."

He smiled for the first time that afternoon. "And to think you didn't even need to pay me," he said, referring to her childhood attempt to buy a kiss.

"Very funny. Consider that kiss a reward."

"What'd I do?"

"You left your room and joined me."

"I did that because I was bored and the smell of the popcorn was too hard to ignore."

"I don't care what brought you back; I'm simply glad you decided to be with me."

"I could leave and come back again," he said, his eyes sparkling.

Addie held on to his gaze before glancing about the

room. "I'm going to need a bit of help deciding where to place the mistletoe. I've heard certain areas of the house offer advantages over others."

"I'm at your service." He urged her toward the archway that led from the entry to the living room. "How about here?"

"Yes, this location looks promising."

Erich brought her into his embrace. "Don't be hasty. We should try it out first. This is an important decision, after all." Before she could comment, he leaned down and kissed her. The kiss they'd exchanged earlier was a prelude to the potency of this one. His arms were heavy on her shoulders, but Addie barely noticed as she tilted back her head and opened to him. The kiss went on until they were both breathless. Erich broke away, his shoulders heaving. He kept his eyes closed.

"Well?" she asked, her voice unsteady. "Should we place it here?"

"It's definitely in the running, but let's not be too quick to make this all-important decision. What about the hall-way?"

Addie laughed softly and tightened her grip around his middle.

"You don't agree?"

"Of course. Location is of great significance."

Erich kissed the tip of her nose. "I feel we should test several rooms. Give each area ample consideration."

Addie gazed up at him, marveling that this thing between them was real. "Can you believe this is happening, Erich?"

"What?"

"Us kissing. I never would have believed it."

"Me neither. I never liked you, you know?"

She didn't need the reminder, especially since the feeling was mutual. "And how do you feel now?"

"And now," he repeated in a whisper. "The truth is, Addie, I can't stop thinking about you. You've changed, I've changed. You're wise and funny, caring, nonjudgmental, and fun. When you're away I wish you were with me, and I wonder how long it will be before I can see you again. I told myself it was the circumstances, my situation, and then I realized I don't care what it is. I like you. I can't help myself. I enjoy your company."

"Really?" Addie was far too tongue-tied to say anything more.

"It's crazy, isn't it?"

"Crazy and wonderful," she agreed. "Now tell me you're happy about the Christmas tree."

The warmth in his gaze faded ever so slightly. "Can't do it, sorry, but I am extremely happy that you're here. The last thing I intend to do when I'm holding you is argue. Now let's test out that mistletoe in another room."

Addie pressed her finger against his lips. "Before we do, I need to ask you something."

He frowned. "Okay, ask, just as long as it doesn't have anything to do with Christmas."

"No, my literature class."

"Ask me later," he murmured, and lowered his head to claim another kiss. All too soon any thoughts or questions were gone from her mind.

Chapter Fifteen

Harry was nervous and uncomfortable. This was an unfamiliar emotion for angels. He wanted to talk to Celeste and share his concerns, but once he did, he was afraid she'd deem it necessary to send him scooting back to heaven. Heaven was wonderful. He wouldn't want to give anyone the wrong impression. It was just that he'd worked so long and hard to earn this position on Earth.

Thankfully, class had gone well, even with the summons to Dr. Conceito's office resting on his desktop. The entire period, Harry had done his best to ignore the request.

Meet me in my office following your class.
President Conceito
Southshore Community College

Harry didn't need to speculate as to the reason he'd been asked to visit the college president's office. He assumed Brady Whitall, the security guard, had gone directly to Dr. Conceito following the disaster the afternoon it'd snowed.

Harry dismissed class. The papers his students had written on the Dickens novel were scattered about his desktop. He lifted a handful and straightened the pile while he mulled over the confrontation awaiting him.

Danny Wade stood in front of the desk. Harry liked the young man. Danny tended to speak his mind and had no qualms about sharing the fact that he'd served time in prison. He seemed to believe his public record earned him a certain amount of respect with his peers.

"Hey, Mr. Mills."

"Yes, Danny?"

Danny was a big guy, tall, with broad shoulders. The tattoo ran halfway down one side of his thick neck. As large as he was, Danny would have excelled if he had turned out for football in high school. Being in sports—part of a team—would have helped him avoid trouble.

"Are you going to take points off for spelling on those papers you had us write? 'Cause I don't spell so good."

"No worries, Danny. Content is more important to me than spelling," he assured him.

"Content? What's content?"

"What you wrote. The meaning behind the words."

Danny rubbed his hand across the back of his neck. "Then why didn't you just say so in the first place? I like this book. It's nothing I would normally read, though."

"So you enjoy reading?"

Danny shrugged. "We got books when I was in prison. I read a few and they were okay, but this Dickens guy . . . he's deep, man. Real deep. He made me think about the stuff I've done and how it's affected others, and it makes me wonder, you know?"

"That's good, Danny."

"I went to see my mama. She's messed up, but I told her I was taking a college class and I could see she was impressed. She didn't ever think one of her kids would go to college. I told her I was gonna make something of myself, and I will."

"I know you will," Harry said, as he collected the remaining papers. "You're doing just fine in this class."

"I never did good in school before, but when Mr. Anderson, he's my parole officer, suggested I take a class, I came to the college. This was the only class that had space available, and I wasn't going to take a class that made me read, but then Mr. Anderson said that it would help me get a job. I'm going to need a job to stay out of trouble, so that was when I decided I was going to do it, so now I'm here."

"That was a good decision. Just keep doing the next right thing, Danny, and you'll be fine."

"I'm doing okay in this class?" His look was almost childlike, his eyes wide and hopeful.

"I'd say you're doing better than okay."

Danny's wide smile was immediate, showing his teeth. "Some in class say I talk too much. You think that, too, Mr. Mills?"

"Not too much," Harry said, carefully choosing his words, unwilling to squelch Danny's enthusiasm. The young man wasn't the least bit shy about sharing his opinions, that was a given. "But it might be a good idea to give others a chance to share once in a while," Harry added.

Danny was completely readable, and some of the excitement left his eyes.

"But I wouldn't want you to stop contributing in class. Your thoughts are impressive and add another layer to our discussion."

The spark returned in Danny's eyes, and Harry was relieved.

"Mr. Mills, being in your class makes me want to open up. It's weird, no teacher's ever done that before." Harry could barely hide his surprise and delight at this comment.

"I was thinking I would bring my mama to the potluck we're having," Danny continued. "She isn't much of a cook, though."

"You bring her, Danny. I'd be happy to meet her, and don't you worry about contributing anything. There's going to be lots of food."

Harry didn't have time to dally long. Keeping Dr. Conceito waiting wasn't a good idea. "Looking forward to meeting her," Harry said, as he reached for his briefcase.

Danny's grin was huge. "Good talking to you, Mr. Mills." Danny tucked the Dickens novel into his coat pocket and headed out the door.

"Good talking to you, too," Harry whispered, as the young man disappeared down the hallway. Danny showed a great deal of promise, and Harry sincerely hoped that God would choose him to guide Danny Wade when the time was right.

Harry draped his coat over his forearm and was ready to leave when he was stopped yet again.

Michelle Heath stood framed in the doorway, holding on to a slip of paper identical to the one Harry had received earlier in the day.

"Oh Harry," she whispered, her face a mask of concern. "This is all my fault. I am so sorry."

"Dr. Conceito wanted to see you, too?" This was bad news. Harry was certain he'd been the only one targeted,

no thanks to Brady Whitall. It went without saying that the
security guard had taken delight in informing the college
president of their infraction against school policy. The janitor might have ratted on her as well.

"I should never have brought the champagne here,"
Michelle continued. "Dr. Conceito has a real thing against
any form of alcoholic beverage on campus grounds. I assumed that since classes were dismissed, we'd be alone
and . . ."

"We'll explain what happened," Harry said, doing his
best to disguise his own concern.

"I would have invited you to my house . . . I should have,
but I didn't think you'd come and so I planned this little
surprise, not realizing. Oh dear, I feel dreadful, just dreadful."

"We aren't children being called to task," Harry said,
and pushed his eyeglasses further up his nose. Although
that was exactly the way he felt—like a child sent to the
principal's office for misbehavior.

"We should go together, don't you think?" Michelle
asked. "And explain."

"Good idea."

Michelle wrapped her arm around his elbow and briefly
leaned her head against his shoulder. "I feel better already,
just talking to you."

"Me, too."

She looked up at him with the roundest, most beautiful eyes he'd ever seen. Her gaze was filled with hope and something else he couldn't read. Admiration? Infatuation? Harry couldn't tell, but whatever it was stirred his blood and the desire to protect her.

"You forgive me, don't you, Harry?"

"There's nothing to forgive." When he first met Michelle, Harry found himself flummoxed by her attention. After that first meeting he recognized that this woman could easily distract him from his mission. On Celeste's advice, he'd avoided Michelle as best he could. The problem was, they saw each other nearly every day, passing in the hallway. Lately it'd become his habit to stop and chat with her a few minutes here and there between classes. In the process, he'd become comfortable with her. Way too comfortable.

Celeste had warned him to avoid anything hinting at romance with a human. It would complicate his mission, possibly compromise it. Harry couldn't allow that to happen, and he wouldn't. Still, he found he'd grown fond of Michelle. He liked the way she tucked her arm around his and leaned her head against his shoulder. It was those human emotions again, warring with his earthly mission.

When Harry and Michelle arrived, Dr. Conceito was

waiting inside his office. They were ushered in and thoroughly lectured. They remained for thirty or more minutes and explained the circumstances. Thankfully, the meeting didn't go as badly as Harry feared. They were reprimanded and then sent on their merry way. Harry realized he would need to tread carefully from this point forward or he might find himself without a job. Then Celeste would have no option but to send him back.

Michelle and Harry parted outside the office. She had things she needed to do, and for that matter, so did he.

Now that the meeting was over, Harry felt he should talk to Celeste. He found her at the coffee stand in the Hub. She wasn't busy when he sidled up to the counter, and while he avoided making eye contact, she focused her attention squarely on him.

Right away, Celeste asked, "How'd the meeting go with Dr. Conceito?"

Harry shrugged. "All right, I guess."

"The news of the two of you is circulating the campus."

"What are people saying?"

"What do you think, Harry?" she asked, sounding concerned. "Word has it that you have a thing for the French teacher and that both of you've been called out. And you already know who started that rumor."

Harry didn't need two guesses. "Brady?"

"Most likely," Celeste concurred. "I wish you'd talked to me before the meeting with Dr. Conceito."

Harry felt her disappointment.

"You don't ever need to be afraid to tell me something," his mentor continued. "I'm here to help with your adjustment in the same way that you're helping your students."

Celeste was right. He should rely on her more.

"So tell me," Celeste said, as she set an Americano on the counter for Harry, "how do you feel after dealing with Dr. Conceito?"

"Better."

Celeste pinned him with a look that had the potential to cut him in half. "Because Michelle went with you?" she asked.

He probably shouldn't admit the truth, but that was unavoidable. "Yes."

"You seem to be falling for her. Are you?" Celeste was nothing if not direct.

Again, lying wasn't an option. "Is that bad?"

"Not really. We are blessed with feelings and emotions. It's all part of being human, even if only for a short time when we're on Earth. The key is learning to adjust. We have to remember that while we might live as humans, we aren't actually human." She paused and studied him for a few moments. "I hope that makes sense."

More and more it did.

"But for Michelle's sake and yours, do not become romantically involved," Celeste warned.

"Duly noted." Harry was more determined than ever to keep his distance from the French teacher, lest he succumb to her charms.

"Now tell me about the potluck," Celeste said.

Harry brightened. It'd been a spur-of-the-moment decision. Classes would be dismissed over Christmas and New Year's but would start up again after the first of the year. The students were just beginning to know one another and become friends. Harry wanted to encourage that. He'd suggested a Christmas potluck and invited the class to bring a favorite dish and a friend to the last session before the break. The response had been enthusiastic.

"Can you come?" he asked.

"If I'm not working."

"I hope you will."

"I'd like that," Celeste said. "It is a good idea. By the way, how is the war veteran in your class working out thus far?"

"Andrew Fairfax?" Harry was concerned about the young man, who had remained silent throughout each session. A number of times Harry had tried to engage him in the discussion. To this point, he'd had little success.

"Andrew is a complicated case," he said, assessing his

student. Harry was anxious to read Andrew's file, which would tell him a lot about where the man was mentally.

"I agree," Celeste said, echoing his thoughts.

"Will I be assigned to help him along with Tommy?" Harry asked. He smiled at the prospect of working alongside an angel who'd taken the form of a dog.

"Not right away. Tommy is his constant companion, but the time is coming when Tommy will leave him. When that happens, it's going to be a rough road for Andrew. I want to be sure you're available then."

"I will be," Harry promised.

"Now give me an update on Addie," Celeste said, and hopped onto a stool on the other side of the counter.

This was by far a more comfortable subject for Harry. Celeste very well knew everything Harry did. What she wanted, he suspected, was his perspective on the situation.

Harry couldn't hold back a grin. "She brought him a Christmas tree, and despite his protests, set it up in his house. Oh, and she tacked up mistletoe. Say, can you explain what it is with mistletoe?" he asked. He'd been meaning to find out but had gotten sidetracked. "Addie and Erich took it from room to room and kissed. I couldn't figure it out. Seems to be potent stuff. Funny, I've never heard of anything like this before now."

The smile on Celeste's face was huge. "I'll explain it later."

"Erich is being stubborn about Christmas," Harry said, continuing the update on the two. "Addie is doing her best to ignore it."

"Addie has come a long way," Celeste said, and sounded pleased.

Harry wished he could take more credit for the changes in his young charge. The truth was, he'd done very little.

"Her father is proud of the changes he sees in her."

"You've talked to her father?" Harry asked, unable to hide his surprise.

"Well, yes. Why else do you think you're here? He was the one who asked for angelic intervention, and God granted his request. It's because of him that you received this assignment."

Harry had had no idea. "Should I do anything about Erich?" he asked.

Celeste sadly shook her head. "Erich isn't your concern. He isn't one of your students. Your ability to influence and guide is available to only those in your class. I'm surprised you need the reminder."

"I didn't . . . I was hoping is all."

"It is a bit of a disappointment. I understand Addie wants him to come to the Christmas potluck, but he refuses. That's unfortunate."

"She's disappointed, but that isn't going to stop her

from attending." Harry was fairly certain she wouldn't allow Erich or his attitude to keep her away.

"It's gratifying to see how well you've worked with Addie," Celeste said, complimenting him. She got very serious then. "Now let's go back to your meeting with Dr. Conceito."

Harry looked down at the hot coffee and pondered his time with the college president. "As you can imagine, he was upset about Michelle and me indulging in a bottle of champagne on school property."

"That's to be expected."

Harry had gotten good news, though. "He said he was willing to make an exception this one time because classes had been dismissed due to the snow." Needless to say, Harry and Michelle had been deeply relieved to have gotten a reprieve.

"But one more instance and . . ."

"One more instance and I am in danger of losing my job," Harry reluctantly admitted.

Celeste sat back and heaved a heavy sigh. "Dr. Conceito is an interesting man," she said, almost as if she was speaking to herself. "He keeps a bottle of bourbon in his bottom desk drawer."

Harry was unable to hide his shock. Dr. Conceito had a drinking problem? "He needs angelic intervention," he said, wondering if the day would come when he would personally receive the assignment.

"He does need help," Celeste agreed, "but right now his heart is too hard for him to be open to the kind of help we can provide. But hopefully that will change."

Chapter Sixteen

Addie was just about to get ready for bed when the lights flickered. She hesitated when it happened again. This time, the lights went out and stayed out. After waiting a couple minutes to see if they came back on, she reached for her phone, turning on the flashlight app, and found her way into the kitchen, where her father always kept the regular flashlight. Thankfully, it was still there.

For most of her growing-up years, Addie had thought of her father as a stuffed shirt, which was probably a term few people used any longer. She'd overheard it once and thought it suited her father perfectly. Now that he was gone she didn't feel nearly as judgmental. In fact, she was grateful he was the kind of person who took care to be so prepared and organized. Finding the flashlight was quick and easy, thanks to his pragmatic nature.

She checked at the window and saw that it wasn't just her house. The entire street was without electricity. Then she wondered about Erich. She'd left him after only a quick visit following class and dinner. He'd been grumpy ever since she'd set up the Christmas tree, which he continued to complain about every visit. As a result, she'd spent less time with him for the last few days. Still, he was her responsibility, and she couldn't ignore him, especially if the power was off.

Addie selected him from her contact list and hoped he had his phone close at hand.

"Hello," he grumbled.

"Hi. You okay?" she asked.

"Is there a reason I shouldn't be?"

She could see his mood hadn't improved. "Are you in bed?"

He hesitated. "No, but I can be if that's what you'd like."

"Very funny."

"Hey, I was serious."

"I'm not playing around," she said. "In case you hadn't noticed, the power's out."

"Yeah, I know."

"Then you're okay?"

Her question was followed by a short pause. "Do you want to come over and hang out?"

"Is that what you'd like?"

He didn't hesitate. "Yes. Do you have your pajamas on?"

"No," she drawled, "but I can put them on if you want me to."

He chuckled. "Come on over."

By all that was right she should ignore him and go back to bed, just the way she'd planned. However, she found his invitation too irresistible to refuse.

"Okay, I'll be there in a few minutes."

The street was coal dark. Thick clouds obliterated any chance of moonlight reflecting off the remaining snow. Without the flashlight, Addie didn't know if she could have walked the short distance between the two homes without incident.

As was her custom, she knocked once and let herself into the house. "Erich?" she called from the entryway.

"In here."

She flashed the light into the living room to find him sitting in the recliner.

"Any idea what happened to cause the power to go out?" he asked.

"It isn't the weather, as far as I can see." The wind or snowfall was often a cause of electrical failures, but the storm had come and gone before they lost power.

"No doubt demand is bigger than supply," he complained. "All these lights. It's ridiculous. Half the street is lit up with decorations. It's a waste of energy."

"Oh, honestly. What is it with you? You weren't like this when we were kids. I'm totally confused by your attitude."

"Don't worry about it."

"What changed, Erich?"

"I grew up. Now sit and hang awhile, okay?"

"First you have to promise no more complaining."

"If it means you'll stay."

"Deal." She hesitated. "Would you like me to build a fire in the fireplace?" That would create a romantic atmosphere and perhaps put Erich in a better mood.

"No thanks."

So much for that. She sat in the chair next to his and gradually relaxed. Addie had missed spending time with him. Refusing to allow him to dominate her time and, more important, her head, had taken some doing. She'd needed time away to put order to her thoughts. This thing with him and Christmas was rooted in something deeper than he was saying. Whatever had happened, he clearly had no intention of sharing with her, and she found that upsetting. They'd come a long way in the last ten days.

They sat in the dark in companionable silence for several minutes. Not being able to see him offered a unique sense of freedom. In a strange way it lowered Addie's walls and allowed her to feel she could be more open, honest, and direct with him.

After a while, Erich said, "I've missed seeing you the last couple days."

So the darkness freed him to share his own feelings with her, too.

"I've been here," she said.

"True, but you were in and out as if you had places to go and people to see. You didn't seem to have much time for me."

It did her heart good to see that Erich had noticed her absence. "Guilty as charged."

"Is it about Christmas?"

"I was tired of hearing you whine. But, yes, the truth is, I also had things to do."

"Like?"

"I went shopping."

"At the mall?" he asked incredulously. "Are you crazy? This time of year it's a madhouse—"

"Grocery shopping," she said, cutting him off, "for the class potluck."

"Ah yes, I forgot about that. Thanks for not bugging me about it."

"I believe you made your decision perfectly clear." It rankled that he'd refused her invitation and hurt her feelings. "As it happened, I asked someone else."

Right away, she could tell he was suspicious. "Who?"

"You don't want to go with me, so it's none of your business."

"Male or female?"

"Does it matter?"

"Yes," he countered sharply. "It matters to me."

"Why?" she asked.

Silence. "Why?" he repeated. "Because I've got a thing for you."

"A thing? Translate, please."

Again he hesitated. "I like you . . . a lot. No one is more surprised over this than I am. For a long time I had trouble believing it, but then you kissed me—"

"Hold on a minute," she said, stopping him. "I kissed you? I sort of thought you were the one who kissed me."

"Getting back to my point."

"Yes," she said, displaying the utmost patience.

"I will if you stop interrupting me."

Addie grinned.

"The point is, I'm falling for you, Addie. I didn't much like it at first."

"Well, thank you ever so much." The man needed a bit of tutoring when it came to giving compliments.

"That didn't come out right. I mean, think about it: We have history, and most of it is negative. And then I had to rely on you for practically everything, which didn't do much for my ego. I wasn't sure what to expect, but frankly, it's been great. Better than great, and it all started about the time we first kissed."

Addie had to agree, it hadn't been easy in the beginning. They'd been tentative with each other, hesitant and unsure. That hadn't lasted long, though, and she was grateful. The only thing that stood between them now was whatever had led to his attitude toward Christmas.

"Do you remember the last time we were in the dark?" Addie asked. She remembered that night all too well. "That was when you told me about Ashley."

The room went silent for the longest time.

"Ah yes, Ashley."

Addie strained harder, fearing she heard longing in his voice as he said the other woman's name. It came to her then what should have been obvious all along—something she'd chosen to ignore. "You're still in love with her, aren't you?"

It took him a minute to admit the truth. "I was at one time, not anymore."

"I don't believe you. You still love her." Addie's stomach felt as though someone had given her a swift, hard kick.

"No," he insisted. "I was honest with you before; for

a time I was crazy about her, and if you must know, I was devastated when she broke up with me. I'd never experienced pain like that." He laughed softly. "Girls had broken up with me more than once, so it was hard to understand why it hit me so much harder this time around. Then I realized it was the way she did it. She waited until she knew I was in really deep and it would cut me to the core."

The thought of Erich loving another woman completely unsettled Addie. She had no right to feel that way—she had no claim on him. But that didn't change how it affected her to hear it. Addie took a moment to absorb this mixed bag of emotions that assailed her.

"No comment?" he asked, after several taut seconds in which neither spoke.

"What would you like me to say?"

He chuckled, his amusement drifting into the darkness like smoke dissipating in the wind. "I'd hoped you'd be insanely jealous."

"That can be arranged."

He laughed again. "Were you this witty when we were kids?"

It hit her then, and she sat up straight as a stick pin. "Hold on a minute," Addie murmured, and placed her hands on top of her head. Everything was starting to add up.

"What?" he asked, sounding concerned.

"Erich, when did Ashley break up with you?"

"Why do you want to know?"

"Just answer the question." She wasn't about to let him get away without answering.

He hesitated and then answered on the tail end of a sigh. "On Christmas Day. We were with family and I got down on one knee to propose and . . . well, you can imagine the rest."

"I knew it. I knew it."

"What did you know?"

"It isn't just *this* Christmas that's got you down. You're still dying for the beautiful Ashley . . . the love of your life. That's the reason you're so negative about the holidays. That's the reason you didn't want me to put up the Christmas tree, or cook a special dinner. You're living in the past, holding on to the memory of a broken heart, hanging on to the pain."

Addie leaped out of the chair. All at once it was much too difficult to sit in one place. For reasons she had yet to digest, she was red-hot angry. "How long do you intend to stay hidden while your heart heals?"

"Ashley and I are finished. When I saw her the other day it was hard for me to believe I could ever have loved her."

"Right, and that was great for your pride, too, wasn't it?"

"Yes, but it was necessary. What I don't understand is why you're so mad."

"You," she cried. "You make me furious. You know what? I don't think I can do this any longer."

"Do what?"

She didn't want to be rash and say something she would later regret. "I think it might be best if I left now. You don't need me."

"You're wrong, Addie. I need you more than ever. I don't understand why you're offended. What did I say? All I know is that I don't want you to leave until we settle this. I did love Ashley, I'll admit it, but it's over. I swear to you it's over."

Addie sucked in a deep breath and exhaled it, torn with what she should do. Before she could decide, the lights on the Christmas tree went on, and flashes of red, blue, and green filled the room, warming it with color.

"The electricity is back," she whispered.

"No, it's not. The lamp and the television are still off. The only lights are the ones on the tree, which I didn't have on to begin with. What's going on?"

Addie glanced out the window, and he was right. The streetlights were still off, and so were the other lights in the neighborhood. Not a one shone in the darkness. The only lights that she could see were those on the Christmas tree.

"That's really strange," she whispered.

"It's more than strange. This isn't possible," he said.

"Maybe it's a sign," Addie suggested.

"Who from?"

"One of the three spirits from the Dickens novel," Addie said, teasing. "I warned you this negative attitude of yours was going to get you in trouble. Well, here you are."

Whatever it was, she would leave him to it. "All I can say is, you're on your own."

He followed her to the front door. "Addie," he whispered, touching her shoulder.

She turned around.

His gaze held her captive. "I don't want you to be angry with me."

"I'm not angry. It just bothers me that you're choosing to hang on to your pain, because it means you're not over Ashley as much as you think."

"Don't be so sure," he murmured, as he reached for her and brought her close. "Kiss me and show me you aren't upset."

"I shouldn't."

"Yes, you should," he insisted, and lowered his mouth to capture hers.

The kiss left her weak in the knees, a kiss that she felt all the way to the soles of her feet. It was as if he had to prove to her in a single kiss that he was completely over the other woman.

"Addie?" he whispered, dragging his mouth reluctantly from hers.

"Hmmm?" she asked, unwilling to open her eyes.

"Will I see you in the morning?"

She nodded. Despite everything she already knew, it would be much too hard for her to stay away.

Chapter Seventeen

With Christmas music playing in the background, Addie slid the last sheet of cookies inside the oven and turned on the timer. She set the oven mitt aside when her phone rang.

As soon as she saw it was Erich, a sense of happiness filled her. She'd taken him breakfast an hour ago, lingering a few minutes while he ate. It'd been a good visit. He'd talked to her a bit more about his relationship with Ashley, opening up to her.

Their talk the night before seemed to have given him a lot to think about.

"I did love Ashley," he'd admitted. "But there's something more I didn't tell you because my pride wouldn't let me. Ashley didn't love me at all. She didn't know what it meant to love one person. She's the kind of woman who will always seek attention from other men, without ever caring for them. The word *faithful* isn't part of her vocabulary."

She hadn't wanted to test his newfound openness, so she'd left before wearing out her welcome.

"Hi," she now greeted him, as she answered the phone.

"What are you doing?" he asked.

"Baking cookies," she reminded him. She'd told him her plans for that morning before she left.

This recipe was one her mother had always baked for the holidays. Peanut butter was one of the main ingredients, and then just before the cookies were completely cooked, she added a chocolate kiss to the top and set them back inside the oven. The chocolate didn't melt completely, but just got gooey and creamy. They'd been her favorite as a kid, and it didn't seem like Christmas without them.

"Don't tell me you miss me already."

"I've had lots of family and friends stop by ever since my accident, but the only person I ever really want to see is you."

"Anyone ever tell you you're a smooth talker?"

"Will my sweet talk earn me any of those cookies you're baking?"

"It might." Addie enjoyed the banter between them. It

seemed good that they could have had such a serious discussion only an hour earlier and then could laugh and tease each other now.

"You still plan on attending that potluck?"

"Yes, what makes you ask?"

He paused. "You never said who you'd asked to join you."

"You're right, I didn't." Mainly because she hadn't actually invited anyone else. Pride insisted she not admit this fact to Erich. Pride could be a demanding master, she'd come to learn.

Then again, Erich had opened up to her that morning. "If you must know . . . I didn't invite anyone else. You're the only person I wanted to bring with me."

The line went still and silent. "I called because I was wondering if it was too late to accept your invitation."

"Because you were jealous?"

"No, because I really do want to come with you . . . okay, and maybe I was a little jealous, but that's not my primary reason."

Addie didn't care what his excuse was. "Oh Erich, I'm so glad. I'd love to have you with me."

"You know what? I think I'm actually going to enjoy this. And you're right. It's time I put this thing I have about Christmas behind me."

"That's great."

He chuckled. "Do I sound anything like Scrooge on Christmas morning?"

"Not quite, but you're getting there."

Several hours later, Addie parked in the school parking lot and hurried around to open the passenger door and help Erich out of her car. He held the plate of cookies in his lap, and she reached for those.

"You didn't bring the entire batch, did you?" he asked.

"No worries, I set aside a dozen for you," she promised.

Right there in the middle of the school parking lot, he rewarded her with a lingering kiss. It took every bit of control Addie possessed not to drop the cookies to the ground and wrap her arms around him.

"Hey, hey," a familiar voice shouted from behind her.

Addie reluctantly broke away from Erich to see Danny walking toward her. At his side was a stylishly dressed woman with a wide-brimmed hat fit for royalty. "Merry Christmas, Danny," she said, feeling a bit sheepish that she'd been caught kissing Erich.

"Yo, Addie. Meet my mother, Tamika. Mom, this is the girl I was telling you about."

Addie looked at the woman, amazed that someone so young could be Danny's mother. "I'm pleased to meet you. Danny's been doing great. He adds a lot to the class."

Danny's eyes beamed with pride. "I told you, Mom. I'm at the head of the class."

Tamika Jackson nodded shyly and stayed close to her son's side.

"Erich Simmons," Erich said, introducing himself. "I'd shake hands, but as you can see it's difficult at the moment."

"I heard about you," Danny said, flashing him a big smile.

"Have you, now?" Erich's gaze shot to Addie.

"Yeah, Addie told me she'd asked you to our party and you turned her down. Glad you decided to come after all."

"I am, too. I've heard lots about you, too."

Danny looked happy. He turned his attention to Addie. "What'd you bring?" he said, eyeing the foil-covered plate.

"Cookies. What about you?"

"Mama don't cook much, and I sure don't, so we stopped off at the store and I got Twinkies."

"Well, it looks like we're going to have plenty of desserts."

"No worries," Danny told her. "Andrew's bringing a pot of chili. His sister made it for him."

"This should be one interesting potluck," Erich mumbled, close to Addie's ear.

"It isn't about the food," Addie whispered back.

The four walked into the building together. Several classmates had already arrived and a table had been set up along one wall, with a paper tablecloth printed with holly and red berries. Addie set down the plate of cookies next to a Crock-Pot full of simmering meatballs. They were covered in what smelled like a hickory-flavored barbecue sauce. Danny proudly opened the box of Twinkies.

The room was soon full. Apparently, Mr. Mills had wanted to make sure he included everyone. Even Elaina, the woman who worked in the cafeteria, was there.

"I have an invitation," she explained, as she set a large plate of tamales in the center of the table. "Mr. Mills invited me and I asked my supervisor and she said I could come as long as my shift was over. I'm not working." She spoke directly to the janitor, Jonas Spelling.

"I'm glad you're here, Elaina," Mr. Mills said, coming up behind the cafeteria worker and placing his hands on her shoulders.

The tamales were piping hot. "I made them fresh."

"Wonderful."

Michelle Heath, who taught the French class down the hall, stopped by with macaroons, though they weren't anything like the coconut ones Addie knew. These looked as if they were made from two meringue cookies pressed together, with filling in the middle.

Just as Danny had said, Andrew arrived with Tommy, with a large pot of chili.

Another woman who wasn't a student was one of the

last to arrive. It took Addie a moment to place her. It was Celeste from the Hub, the woman who worked at the latte stand. She brought scones, adding to the assortment of desserts.

The desks had been shifted about until they formed a circle. Mr. Mills stood in the center of the room and asked for their attention. "Before we fill our plates, I'd like everyone to go around the room and introduce themselves and their guests."

They started with Danny, who was generally the first to speak up. "Everyone knows I'm Danny and this is my mama," he said with pride, as he placed his arm around his mother's shoulders. "She won't say much."

"She won't need to, with you doing all the talking for her," someone called out, and the rest of the class laughed.

The two young high school students went next. Addie had barely spoken to either one and made a mental note to get to know them better after the first of the year.

When it was her turn, she introduced Erich. "Erich and I grew up next door to each other."

"We weren't always friendly," Erich went on to explain. "It's only been in the last couple weeks that we've learned to get along." He smiled at Addie.

"Now they're really getting *friendly*," Danny announced. "I ran into them making out in the parking lot."

Everyone laughed and clapped.

When it was the janitor's turn, he stepped forward. "Jonas Spelling. Most of you won't recognize me without me holding my broom. I'm here at Mr. Mills's invitation. I wasn't sure about him when he first arrived, but he keeps a clean classroom. I take my job as custodian seriously. I have custody of this building. It's my responsibility."

Elaina blushed when it was her turn, and she spoke in Spanish until she looked at the confused faces of those around her. "I'm sorry," she said in English. "I forget to speak English when I'm nervous. I work in the cafeteria, and Mr. Mills invited me, too."

"I invited the security guard, too, but he was unable to attend," added Mr. Mills.

"He's probably cleaning his gun," muttered Michelle Heath, under her breath. Addie was fairly certain she wasn't supposed to hear.

"Before we help ourselves to this fine meal," Mr. Mills said, "I'd like to say what a pleasure it is to have each one of you in the class. You've welcomed and encouraged me. Merry Christmas and God bless."

"Merry Christmas," the group echoed back.

As they formed a line at the table, Addie thought she caught sight of someone outside the window, attempting to look inside. But when she went to gaze outside, she couldn't see anyone.

Erich joined her. "What are you looking for?"

"Nothing," she assured him. "I thought I saw someone." It was probably her imagination. Anyone who wanted to come into the building was welcome. The doors weren't locked.

"I understand now why you've enjoyed this class so much. They're cool."

Addie's gaze drifted around the room. They'd started out as strangers and had become her friends. "They're great. I love Danny's enthusiasm, and I've got a soft spot for Andrew."

"Do you have a soft spot for me?" Erich asked, holding her look.

She offered him an affectionate smile. "Not in the same way. Do you remember what you told me the other day?" she asked, and then elaborated. "What you said about thinking about me all the time and missing me when I wasn't there?"

"I meant every word."

"The thing is, I feel the same way about you, Erich. It bothered me that you refused to enjoy Christmas because of an old girlfriend."

"I think I'm finally getting over it. Remember last night when the power went out?"

Addie wasn't likely to forget. "Of course."

"When the tree lights came on and nothing else did, I realized how stupid I've been. The thing is . . ." He hesitated and looked around the room, then lowered his voice.

"The thing I realized," he said, starting again, "is that if Ashley was in my life I would never have had this time with you. I wouldn't have ever known what an amazing woman you are."

"Does this mean you're going to stop complaining and start enjoying the holiday?" she asked.

"Bring on the holiday cheer. This Scrooge has had a change of heart."

Addie laughed and leaned her head against his shoulder. "What will our mothers think once they're back from the cruise, I wonder?" she asked.

"I can't speak for yours . . . mine is going to be excited."

"Mine, too," Addie assured him. "I realize that in a few weeks everything will be different. The casts will be off and you obviously won't be dependent on me or anyone else anymore."

"My feelings for you aren't going to change."

"You can't be sure of that," she said. "I understand, I mean . . ."

"Addie." He turned her around and held her look prisoner. "The only thing that's going to change is that I'll return to my own condo. I assumed after Ashley that I'd never be able to feel this deeply about another woman again. You proved me wrong. In case you haven't figured it out yet, I'm really crazy about you."

Addie swore her heart swelled to twice its normal size

just hearing those words. "I've fallen pretty hard for you, too."

A slow, easy smile slid into place. "Where's the mistletoe when you need it?" Erich complained.

"I don't think we need mistletoe," she whispered.

His gaze held hers for the longest moment, and it felt as if she could melt into a puddle. Falling for Erich was the biggest surprise of her life. She wasn't sure where it would lead or if it would last. One thing she did know: This was bound to be one of the best Christmases of her life.

Epilogue

"That was a lovely party," Celeste said, after everyone had cleared the classroom and only the two of them remained.

Harry agreed. "I think Addie and Erich have had a breakthrough."

"I do as well," Celeste agreed. "You helped quite a bit, with her and with Erich."

Harry murmured noncommittally.

"I know about the Christmas tree lights, Harry."

"You do?" He knew he was skirting the edge of what was acceptable, since they'd really been designed to help Erich over his hurdle. But they'd been for Addie, too, and therefore could be justified. He waited for Celeste to reprimand him, but she didn't.

"I believe Addie has started down the right path now. She's happier than she's been in a good long while. It took courage for her to pack up her life and return home. It meant admitting she was wrong and doing an abrupt about-face. Before she could grow as a person, she needed to learn to temper her stubbornness, and she has."

"Yes, she really did it. She has plans to continue with classes, and she wants to get into the medical field."

"Like her father," Harry murmured. "That's fitting, isn't it?"

"She will shine when it comes to dealing with patients."

"Again, like her father, right?" Harry asked.

"Yes. Only recently has she come to recognize how alike they are."

Harry agreed as he started to straighten the desks, using that as a distraction so he wouldn't have to look at Celeste as he said, "I hope you didn't mind that I invited Michelle." Celeste had certainly given him enough warnings when it came to a relationship with the French teacher, and he assumed his mentor would be annoyed that he'd invited her.

"Not at all," she surprised him by answering. "You need friends on the faculty, Harry."

"I'll be careful not to allow matters to progress beyond friendship."

Celeste nodded. "That would be wise." She walked over to the far side of the room near the windows. "I don't suppose you noticed Dr. Conceito."

Harry stiffened with alarm. "He stopped by?"

"Not exactly."

Frowning, Harry asked, "What does that mean?"

"He was outside, peeking in the window."

"Dr. Conceito?"

"No worries. I can promise you that all he saw was you teaching class just as you would any other day."

"But—"

"Brady Whitall told him about the potluck. You probably aren't aware that holding functions such as this potluck is strictly against school policy."

"The handbook doesn't say anything about—"

"It's in the small print. It's one of Dr. Conceito's little tricks," Celeste informed him.

"Why peek in the window when he could have walked right into the classroom?"

"He didn't want to do that."

"Why not?"

"Dr. Conceito wanted to see who was attending the party before he raised a fuss. He didn't want to offend an ally."

"You mean someone like Jonas?" It'd surprised and gladdened Harry's heart that the custodian had shown up.

"Exactly."

"But regardless, when Dr. Conceito looked . . ."

"There was no party," Celeste assured him.

Harry's shoulders sagged with relief.

"I wonder if you picked up on something else going on at the party."

Plenty of sharing and laughter had taken place, but Harry wasn't sure what Celeste meant. "What?"

His mentor looked rather pleased with herself. "Jonas and Elaina."

"What about them?" Harry had done his best to spend time with each of his students and exchange greetings with their guests. Preoccupied as he was, he didn't get a chance to notice anything else.

"Jonas helped himself to a second tamale and complimented Elaina. You should have seen her blush. Then they got to talking. I think you might find him more of an ally than an adversary in the upcoming weeks."

"Really?" This was an interesting development.

"What are your feelings about Danny?" Celeste asked.

Harry had given plenty of thought to the young parolee. "Danny's got a good heart. All we need to do is keep him on track. He has tremendous potential."

"I agree," Celeste concurred. "You've done well, Harry. You've adjusted to human emotions and have come to love these humans just as God intended."

His heart raced as he asked, "Does this mean I'll be able to continue with my work here on Earth?"

"I believe there's a very good possibility that you will."

This was the best news Harry could have gotten. Oh yes, just as Addie had thought. This was going to be the best Christmas ever.

If *Mr. Miracle* had you believing
in the magic of the holidays, you won't want to miss

Starry Night

filled with Debbie Macomber's signature blend
of romance and Christmas cheer.
Read on for a sneak peek.

Available from Ballantine Books

Chapter One

Carrie Slayton's feet were killing her. She'd spent the last ninety minutes standing in two-inch heels at a charity art auction in a swanky studio in downtown Chicago. She couldn't understand how shoes that matched her black dress so beautifully could be this painful. Vanity, thy name is fashion.

"My name is spelled with two *l*'s," the middle-aged woman, dripping in diamonds, reminded her. "That's Michelle, with two *l*'s."

"Got it." Carrie underlined the correct spelling. Michelle, spelled with two *l*'s, had just spent thirty thousand dollars for the most ridiculous piece of art Carrie had ever seen. True, it was for a good cause, but now she seemed to feel her name needed to be mentioned in the news article Carrie would write for the next edition of the *Chicago Herald*.

"It would be wonderful to have my husband's and my picture to go along with your article," Michelle added. "Perhaps you should take it in front of the painting."

Carrie looked over her shoulder at Harry, the photographer who'd accompanied her from the newspaper.

"Of course, Lloyd and I would want approval of any photograph you choose to publish."

"Of course," Carrie said, doing her best to keep a smile in place. If she didn't get out of these shoes soon, her feet would be permanently deformed. She wiggled her toes, hoping for relief. Instead they ached even worse.

Harry, bless his heart, dutifully stepped forward, camera in hand, and flashed two or three photos of the couple posing in front of what might have been a red flower or a painting of a squished tomato or possibly the aftermath of a murder scene. Carrie had yet to decide which. The title of the work didn't offer a clue. *Red.* Yes, the painting was in that color, but exactly what it depicted remained a mystery.

"Isn't it stunning?" Michelle asked when she noticed Carrie staring at the canvas.

Carrie tilted her head one way and then another, looking for some clue as to its possible significance. Then, noticing that Michelle, spelled with two *l*'s, was waiting for her response, she said, "Oh, yes, it's amazing."

Harry didn't bother to hide his smile, knowing that all Carrie really wanted was to get out of those ridiculous shoes. And to think she'd gotten her journalism degree for this!

Carrie knew she was fortunate to have a job with such a prestigious newspaper. A professor had pulled a favor and gotten her the interview. Carrie had been stunned when she'd been hired. Surprised and overjoyed.

Two years later, she was less so. Her assignment was the society page. When she was hired, she'd been told that eventually she'd be able to write meatier pieces, do interviews and human-interest stories. To this point, it hadn't happened. Carrie felt trapped, frustrated, and underappreciated. She felt her talent was being wasted.

To make matters worse, her entire family lived in the Pacific Northwest. Carrie had left everything she knew and loved behind, including Steve, her college sweetheart. He'd married less than six months after she took the position in Chicago. It hadn't taken him long, she noted. The worst part was that Carrie was far too busy reporting on social events to have time for much of a social life herself. She dated occasionally, but she hadn't found anyone who made her heart race. Dave Schneider, the man she'd been seeing most recently, was more of a friend than a love interest. She supposed after Steve she was a bit hesitant to get involved again. Maybe once she left the *Herald* and moved home to write for a newspaper in the Seattle area, like she planned, things would be different.

Back inside her condo, Carrie gingerly removed her shoes and sighed with relief.

This was it. She was done. First thing in the morning she would hand in her two-week notice, sublet her condo, and take her chances in the job market in Seattle. If the managing editor, Nash Jorgen, refused to give her the opportunity to prove she had what it took, then why stay? She refused to be pigeonholed.

That decided, Carrie limped into her bedroom and fell into bed, tired, frustrated, and determined to make a change.

"You can't be serious," argued Sophie Peterson, her closest friend at the newspaper, when Carrie told her of her decision.

"I'm totally serious," she said as she hobbled to her desk.

"What's wrong with your foot?" Sophie asked, tagging behind her.

"Stupidity. This gorgeous pair of shoes was only available in a half-size smaller than what I normally wear. They were so perfect, and they were buy one pair, get the second half off. I couldn't resist, but now I'm paying for it."

"Carrie, don't do it."

"Don't worry, I have no intention of wearing those heels again. I tossed them in a bag for charity."

"Not that," Sophie argued. "Don't hand in your notice! You're needed here."

"Not as a reporter," Carrie assured her, dumping her purse in her bottom drawer and shucking off her thick winter coat. "Sorry, my mind is made up. You and I both know Nash will never give me a decent assignment."

"You're your own worst enemy." Sophie leaned against the wall that separated their two cubicles and crossed her arms and ankles.

"How's that?"

"Well, for one thing, you're the perfect fit for the society page. You're drop-dead gorgeous, tall, and thin. It doesn't hurt that you look fabulous in a slinky black dress and a pair of spike heels. Even if I could get my hair to grow that thick, long, and curly without perming the living daylights out of it, Nash would never consider someone like me. It isn't any wonder he wants you on the job. Give the guy a little credit, will you? He knows what he's doing."

"If looks are the only criterion—"

"There's more," Sophie said, cutting her off. "You're great with people. All you need to do is bat those baby blues at them and strangers open up to you. It's a gift, I tell you, a real gift."

"Okay, I'm friendly, but this isn't the kind of writing I want to do. I've got my heart set on being a reporter, a real reporter, writing about real news and interesting people." In the beginning, Carrie had been flattered by the way people went out of their way to introduce themselves at the events she covered. It didn't take long for her to recognize that they were looking for her to mention their names in print. What shocked her was the extent people were willing to go in order to be noticed. She was quickly becoming jaded, and this bothered her even more than Nash's lack of faith in her abilities.

The holidays were the worst, and while it was only early November, the frenzy had already started. The list of parties Nash assigned her to attend was already mammoth. Halloween decorations were still arranged around her desk, and already there was a Christmas tree in the display window of the department store across the street.

Determined to stick with her plan, Carrie went directly into Nash Jorgen's office.

A veteran newsman, Nash glanced up from his computer screen and glared in her direction. He seemed to sense this wasn't a social visit. His shoulders rose with a weary sigh. "What now?" he growled.

"I'm handing in my two-week notice." If she'd been looking for a response, she would have been disappointed.

He blinked a couple of times, ran his hand down the side of his day-old beard, and asked, "Any particular reason?"

"I hoped to prove I can be a darn good reporter, but I'll never get the chance writing anything more than copy for society weddings. You said when you hired me that you'd give me a shot at reporting real news."

"I don't remember what I said. What's wrong with what you're writing now? You're good."

"It isn't what I want to write."

"So? You make the best of it, pay your dues, and in time you'll get the break you're looking for."

Carrie was tired of waiting. She straightened her shoulders, her resolve tightening. "I know I'm fortunate to work for the *Herald*. It was a real coup to get this position, but this isn't the career I wanted. You give me no choice." She set her letter of resignation on his desk.

That got Nash's attention. He swiveled his chair around to look at her once more. His frown darkened, and he ran his hand through his thinning hair. "You really are serious, aren't you?"

A chill went down her spine. Nash was actually listening. "Yes, I'm serious."

"Fine, then." He reached across his desk and picked up a hardcover book and handed it to her. "Find Finn Dalton, get an interview, and write me a story I can print."

She grabbed hold of the book, not recognizing the author's name. "And if I do?"

"Well, first, there's a snowball's chance of you even locating him. Every reporter in the universe is dying to interview him. But if you get lucky and he's willing to talk and we print the piece, then I'll take you off the society page."

Carrie wavered. He seemed to be offering her a chance, as impossible as it might seem. Now it was up to her to prove herself. She dared not show him how excited she was. "I'll find him."

He snickered as though he found her confidence amusing, and then sobered. He regarded her with the same dark frown he had earlier before a slow, easy smile slid over his harsh features. "I bet you will. Now, listen up—if you get an interview with Finn Dalton, you can have any assignment you want."

Taking small steps, Carrie backed out of the office. She pointed at Nash. "I'm holding you to your word."

The managing editor was already back to reading his computer screen and didn't appear to have heard her. It didn't matter; she'd heard him, and he'd come across loud and clear.

Once she was out of his office, she examined the book to see the author photo, but couldn't find one, not even on the inside back flap.

Walking back to her cubicle, she paused at Sophie's instead. "You ever heard of Finn Dalton?"

Sophie's eyebrows lifted on her round face. "You mean you haven't?"

"No." The book title wasn't much help. *Alone.* That told her next to nothing. The jacket revealed a snow-covered landscape with a scattering of stubby trees.

Sophie shook her head. "Have you been living under a rock?"

"No. Who is this guy?"

"He's a survivalist who lives alone someplace in the Alaskan wilderness."

"Oh." That was a bit daunting, but Carrie considered herself up to the challenge. She'd been born and raised in Washington State. She'd hoped to join her family for Thanksgiving, but if she needed to use her vacation time to find Finn Dalton, then she was willing to.

"His book has been on the bestseller lists for nearly seven months, mostly at the number-one position."

Carrie was impressed. "What does he write about?"

"He's the kind of guy you can set loose in the wild with a pack of chewing gum, a pocketknife, and a handkerchief, and by the time you find him he's built a shelter and a canoe. From what I've read, his stories about Alaskan life and survival in the tundra would kink your hair. Well, not that yours needs curling."

This was Sophie's idea of a joke. Carrie's wild dark brown curls were the bane of her existence. She tamed them as best she could, but she often found herself the brunt of jokes over her out-of-control hair.

"Nash says he doesn't give interviews."

"Not just doesn't give interviews—this guy is like a ghost. No one has ever met or even talked to him."

"Surely his publisher or his editor—"

"No," Sophie said, cutting her off. "Everything has been done by computer."

"Well, then . . ."

"All anyone knows is that he lives near an Alaskan lake somewhere in the vicinity of the Arctic Circle."

"How is it you know so much about this guy?"

"I don't, and that's just it. No one does. The press has gone wild looking for him. Plenty of reporters have tried to track him down, without success. No one knows how to find him, and Finn Dalton doesn't want to be found. He should have called his book *Leave Me Alone*. Someone could pass him on the street and never know it was him, and from everything I've read, that's exactly how he likes it."

Intrigued, Carrie flipped through the pages of the book. "Nash said I could have any assignment I wanted if I got an interview from Finn Dalton."

"Of course he did. Nash has been around long enough to know he's got you in a no-win situation."

Carrie glanced up. "I don't care. I'm going to try."

"I hate to be a killjoy here, but, Carrie, no way will you find this guy. Better reporters than either of us have tried and failed. Every newspaper, magazine, and media outlet is looking to dig up information about him, without success. Finn Dalton doesn't want to be found."

That might be the case, but Carrie refused to give up without even trying. This was far too important to drop just because it was a long shot. "I'm desperate, Sophie." And really, that said it all. If she was going to have a real career in journalism, she had to find Finn Dalton. Her entire future with the *Chicago Herald* hung in the balance.

"I admire your determination," Sophie murmured, "but I'm afraid you're going to hit one dead end after another."

"That might be the case." Carrie was willing to admit to her friend that finding Finn Dalton wouldn't be easy. "But I refuse to quit without trying." She knew Sophie didn't mean to be negative. "I want this chance, and if it means tracking Finn Dalton into some forsaken tundra, then I will put on my big-girl shoes and go for it." But not the heels she'd worn last night, that was for sure.

The first thing Carrie did in her search for Finn Dalton was read the book. Not once, but three times. She underlined everything that gave her a single hint as to his identity.

For two days she skipped lunch, spending her time on the computer, seeking any bit of information she could find that would help her locate Finn Dalton. She went from one search engine to another.

"How's it going?" Sophie asked as they met each other on their way out the door a couple of days later.

"Good." Through her fact-finding mission, Carrie was getting a picture of the man who had written this amazing book. After a third read she almost felt as if she knew him. He hadn't always been a recluse. He'd been raised in Alaska and had learned to live off the land from his father, whom he apparently idolized. One thing was certain, he seemed to have no use for women. In the entire book, not once did he mention his mother or any other female influence. It was more of what he didn't say that caught Carrie's attention.

"Any luck?" Sophie asked, breaking into her thoughts.

"Not yet." She hesitated. "Have you read the book?"

Sophie nodded. "Sure. Nearly everyone has."

"Did you notice he has nothing to say about the opposite sex? I have the feeling he distrusts women."

Sophie shrugged as if she hadn't paid much notice, but then she hadn't been reading between the lines the way Carrie had.

"How old do you think he is?" Sophie asked.

"I can't really say." Finn was an excellent writer and storyteller. But the tales he relayed could have happened at nearly any point in the last several decades. Current events were skipped over completely.

Sophie crossed her arms and looked thoughtful. "My guess is that he's fifty or so, to have survived on his own all these years."

Speculation wouldn't do Carrie any good. "Tell you what. When I find out, you'll be the first to know. Deal?"

Sophie smiled and nodded. "Deal."

That night, as Carrie readied for her latest charity event, her cell rang. It was her mother in Seattle. They spoke at least two or three times a week. Carrie was tight with her family and missed them dreadfully.

"Hi, Mom," she answered, pressing her cell to one ear while she attempted to place a pearl earring in her other earlobe.

"Hi, sweetheart. Are you busy?"

"I've got a couple of minutes." She switched ears and stabbed the second pearl into place before tucking her feet into a comfortable pair of high heels. She was scheduled to meet Harry in thirty minutes.

"Dad and I are so excited to see you at Thanksgiving."

"Yes, about that." Carrie grabbed her purse and tucked it under her arm while holding on to her phone. "Mom, I hate to tell you this, but there's a possibility I might not make it home for Thanksgiving."

"What?"

The disappointment in her mother's voice was painful to hear. "Have you ever heard of Finn Dalton?"

"Oh, sure. Your father loved his book so much he bought two additional copies. I read it, too. Now, that's a man."

"I want to interview him."

"Really? From what I understand, he doesn't give interviews."

"Yeah, that's what I heard, too."

"Does he ever come to Chicago?"

"Doubtful," Carrie murmured. If only it could be that easy and he would come to her. Well, that wasn't likely. Then again, something Sophie said had stayed in her mind. She could walk past him on the sidewalk and never know it was him. "I'll need to track Finn Dalton down, but I keep running into dead ends the same as everyone else." She mentioned her online search, the calls to Alaska, and the number of phones slammed in her ear. No one had been willing to talk to her. "I have to look at this from a different angle. Have you got any ideas?"

"From what your father said, Finn Dalton isn't a man who would enjoy being written up on the society page."

"That's just it, Mom. This would be an investigative piece. My editor told me I could have my pick of assignments if I was able to get this interview. It's important, enough for me to take the vacation days I planned to use for Thanksgiving to find him."

"Oh, Carrie, I hate the thought of you doing that."

"I know, I hate it, too, but it's necessary." Her mother was well aware of Carrie's feelings toward her current work situation.

"Do you really think you can find Finn Dalton?" her mother asked.

"I don't know if I can or not, but if I don't, it won't be for lack of trying."

"I've always admired your tenacious spirit. Can I tell your father you're going to write a piece on the man who wrote *Alone*?"

"Ah . . . not yet. I have to locate Dalton first."

"What have you discovered so far?" Her mother was

nothing if not practical. Carrie could visualize her mother pushing up her shirtsleeves, ready to tackle this project with Carrie.

"Do you know where he was born?"

"No. I assumed it must have been Alaska, but there's no record of his birth there. I've started going through the birth records of other states, starting with the northwest, but haven't found his name yet." At this rate, it would be the turn of the next century before she found the right Dalton.

"What about his schooling? Graduation records?"

"I tried that, but he's not listed anywhere. Maybe he was homeschooled."

"You're probably right," her mother said, sounding proud that Carrie had reasoned it out. "One of his stories mentions his father mailing away for books, remember? Those were textbooks, I bet."

Carrie had made the same assumption.

"Finn is a rather unusual name, isn't it?" her mother continued softly, as though she was thinking out loud.

"And of course it could be a pseudonym, but his publisher claims the name is as real as the man." Nothing seemed the norm when it came to Finn Dalton.

"You know, work on the Alaskan pipeline was very big about the time your father and I got married. That was a huge project, and it brought a lot of men to Alaska; many of them stayed. His father might have been one of them."

"Yes." But that was a stab in the dark. She'd already spent hours going over every type of record she could think to research from Alaska, to no avail. Carrie glanced at the time, even though this talk was helping her generate ideas of where to continue looking for the mysterious Mr. Dalton.

"From what I remember, a lot of men left their wives and families for the attraction of big money."

"I could start looking at the employment records for the pipeline from that time period and see what I find," Carrie said.

"That's a terrific idea. And listen, when you find Finn Dalton, make sure your dad gets a chance to chat with him, would you?"

"I can't promise that." First she'd need to convince Finn Dalton to talk to her!

"Just do your best."

"I'll do what I can."

"Bye, sweetie."

"Bye, Mom." Carrie ended the call and dumped her cell in her small bag. After a quick glance in the hallway mirror, she headed out the door to what she hoped would be one of the very last social events she would ever need to cover.

ABOUT THE AUTHOR

DEBBIE MACOMBER, the author of *Love Letters, Blossom Street Brides, Starry Night, Rose Harbor in Bloom, Starting Now, Angels at the Table,* and *The Inn at Rose Harbor,* is a leading voice in women's fiction. Nine of her novels have hit #1 on the *New York Times* bestseller list, with three debuting at #1 on the *New York Times, USA Today,* and *Publishers Weekly* lists. In 2009 and 2010, *Mrs. Miracle* and *Call Me Mrs. Miracle* were Hallmark Channel's most-watched movies for the year. In 2013, Hallmark Channel produced the original series *Debbie Macomber's Cedar Cove.* She has more than 170 million copies of her books in print worldwide.

ABOUT THE TYPE

This book was set in Sabon, a typeface designed by the well-known German typographer Jan Tschichold (1902–74). Sabon's design is based upon the original letter forms of sixteenth-century French type designer Claude Garamond and was created specifically to be used for three sources: foundry type for hand composition, Linotype, and Monotype. Tschichold named his typeface for the famous Frankfurt typefounder Jacques Sabon (c. 1520–80).